Just Another Girl's Story

A Memoir on Finding Redemption

Laura Eckert

Author's Note: This book is non-fiction. It is written honestly and to the best reconciliation of the author. To protect the privacy of certain individuals, some names have been changed.

All Scripture references are taken from *Couples Devotional Bible: New International Version.* (1994). Grand Rapids, MI: Zondervan Pub. House.

Just Another's Girls Story / Laura Eckert / First Edition
ISBN-13: 978-1541198456
ISBN-10: 154119845X
Library of Congress Control Number: 2017907863
CreateSpace Independent Publishing Platform, North Charleston, SC

Dedications

To my daughter. In 1986 you changed my life and gave me purpose. You are kind, generous and love hard. You are everything I hoped you would be. You have given me great strength when I wanted to let my demons win.

To my husband. For all that we've been through, the joy, the tragedy and everything in between, at the end of every day my heart is forever yours. You have been my biggest fan and have always given me the space I need to go after my dreams.

To my son. You are the epitome of perseverance and tradition. Your example of accepting all people for whom they are, helps to keep me grounded and grateful that you have such a warm and loving heart. In your adulthood, you have become one of my most precious confidants.

To my mom. Lord knows the pain and turmoil I put you through over the years. Your examples of strength and dedication gave me the foundation that I used when I became a mother. You never gave up on me and always made sure that I knew no matter what I did, you couldn't love me any less, only more.

Lastly, to my very special aunt. You've been a second mom to me and always went above and beyond to save me throughout my teenage years. You gave me a home and was my living guardian angel that loved me unconditionally. I will forever be grateful.

I am not who I used to be.

Contents

Foreword by Kim Carr

Laura and I go back quite a way, and I've seen two very different sides of her. Once we were housemates; later, bitter enemies and now we are dear and trusted friends. We have a shared history, shared hurts, but more than that we share an understanding of true redemption and a relationship with the amazing God who offers it so freely.

Transformative love is the simplest way to describe redemption. Laura Eckert, my amazing, beautiful friend has run the gamut when it comes to transformation! As you will read in the pages to come, there is no one and no act that is beyond redemption.

This very book is a reflection of that change in Laura. You see, secrets and addictions can't thrive and fester their poison when thrust into the light. In bringing her story and the story of her family to light, it is also an opportunity to help others avoid some heartache or for others living with shame or regret to bury their fears and boldly walk into the light that allows the freedom of God's love to transform them as well.

As you read these pages, you will learn some very shocking things, but I hope you continue to read on to the end. You will be blessed with a better understanding of redemption and the miracle that is in it.

PART ONE
ABRIDGED

CHAPTER ONE

Righteous

Who could disagree that if God is at the center of your life, you can never make a wrong decision? Right? Well, this is what I came to believe after surviving my teenage years, so much so that by my mid-thirties, I sat on a high horse that was so tall, no one could reach up and touch me. I was on the right side of any controversial issue whether it be sex before marriage, the right to life, and even the death penalty. I had it covered, and I schooled anyone who dared challenge me.

Raging anger would brew to the top of my ego as I would hiss, "You're wrong! How can you not see the truth in this?" Then I would yell, "Stop arguing with me and start listening!"

When deep in the throes of a heated debate, I demanded to know why my perceived enemy could not understand my point of view. By then I never failed in firmly placing God at the center of all my arguments, and those who didn't see eye to eye with me wound up on my "THIS PERSON IS AN IDIOT LIST." Once this happened, I couldn't take them seriously, and I'd steer clear of any future discussion with them... controversial or not.

How did I get here? I made a lot of messes in my teenage years. I lost my virginity at the age of 14. At age 16 I had my first abortion. At age 17, I had my second abortion. At age 19, I had my first baby. All of these significant events changed me; for worse and then for better.

CHAPTER TWO

I'll Take the

Blame

Right through my 20s and into my early 30s, I was flying by the seat of my pants. It was how I had always run my young life. More to the point, I was escaping reality in the throes of a sexual addiction, and it was ruining my young life.

The only time "caution" meant anything to me was when it came to my appearance. I was mindful to pick low-calorie foods to be skinny (like the models in Seventeen Magazine), wear clothes that were in vogue, make-up that made me look like those models (or so I thought), and the right color hair dye to bring it all together. These were my top priorities. Oh, and having sex with my step-brother topped the list as well.

Insignificant in comparison to those things were the friends I gravitated to, the language I spoke, and how I treated my family. I didn't give a single thought to real life consequences.

Regretfully, it took me too many moons to grow up; far longer than for most is my guess. I was too busy playing the blame game with my parents. They were my perceived combatants. I blamed them for a lousy upbringing, for the black cloud always hanging over my head, and the sadness that made me cry because all I wanted to be was normal like my friends. I mostly blamed them for my abortions.

In my mind, they made me have them, so all the suffering and shame eating me alive was their doing. My parents should have known better. I was dependent on their reign over me. They were the adults in the room, not me. Yet, I suffered the consequences of their adult decisions over my life.

At a time when my family became a blended family, I'd hear people compare us to the Brady Bunch television show. Three boys, three girls, mom, and dad. With the exception of Alice, the live-in housekeeper, we did fit that bill. We even had the dog, but instead of being named Tiger, ours was named Buffy.

However, the Brady Bunch show was family values fiction, and our family life was nothing like that. Instead, one could compare the MTV reality show, 16 and Pregnant to our family; or at least to me.

My mom and step-dad were no Mike and Carol Brady; this is for certain. They were either blind or naïve. Either one helped to set the stage for a family life that was far different from the Brady Bunch Show.

We never learned what Religion the Brady family followed if any, but I was raised Catholic, and my teenage behaviors were unbecoming of the values taught in my adolescence.

By the time I reached my mid-thirties, I had decided the crap I'd been through wasn't my parents' fault after all, per se. Yeah, their marriage blended us together. Yes, they drove me to the abortion clinics and paid for the *procedures*. But no, they did not force me into a sex addiction with my step-brother. I am sure they would rather we emulated Peter and Jan Brady, the middle-kids of the Brady clan that awkwardly got along and never desired each other sexually. However, that was not to be.

Akin to a "Come to Jesus Moment," I was moved over a short period to stop acting like a brat and take responsibility for my past. Then, bam! I got it. I was responsible, no one else. Several situations brought me to this new way of thinking; mainly church, college, and mission trips. My husband and children were responsible too. The order of impact is not as important as the actual destination I reached – redemption.

My husband and I have two kids, a boy and a girl. We raised them as Catholics, like us, but more aggressively. We were like drill sergeants, enforcing strict rules attached with consequences we rarely faced in our youth. Our quest was to provide enough structure to keep them out of trouble, but also give them some wiggle room to be kids and giggle and make happy memories. Happy memories of my youth are hard for me to come by and I desperately wanted my children to have them.

We aimed high and hard to be as righteous as we could. Admittedly, it was I who aimed the most at such a hard reaching pursuit. Always needing to be one thousand times better than my past, I peppered acts of righteousness in almost everything we did as a family. If a movie wasn't rated PG or G, it was off-limits. TV shows like South Park and Friends were prohibited, none of that "smut" was allowed in our home.

We went to church every Sunday and sat close to the front. This way, the kids could fully engage in Mass and hopefully get something from the Sermon. I hoped for something more than I ever did. As a kid, I thought that Mass was boring, and I always fidgeted in the pew, never able to sit in comfort because of the hard wooden benches under my bony rear-end.

In their teen years, I made sure the kids were clear that sex before marriage was forbidden. In fact, both declared a purity pledge and had rings to prove they would wait until being wed. If I could help it, they would not suffer as their parents had, with unplanned pregnancies. Someday they would thank us, so I believed.

Even though we ran a tight ship, we had a lot of fun too. I guess you could liken us to the television show, 7th Heaven with a dose of Everybody Loves Raymond. We spent boatloads of time with our extended family, which for us, was *our* parents and *our* brothers and sisters. You see, at age 22, I married my step-brother, Shawn. Our unique marriage gave way to interesting family gatherings in the beginning. Over time, though, our relationship became old hat.

In my early 30s, I was in graduate school and on the verge of collecting another piece of paper which exclaimed: "I'm educated and smart." For me, it meant I had succeeded in overcoming a lackluster opinion of myself about how intelligent I was. I blew my entire high school education caring only about my outer self and never took the time to realize that I might have had a brain; capable of real intelligence.

Once I discovered I had some smarts, I became pretty darn confident. Thus, the aforementioned attitude. From the beginning of college, I was hell bent to prove I could be studious and get good grades. No more Fs for this girl. In fact, no other grade but an A would do. I was not going to be labeled "one of those girls" who let her past prevent her from getting some letters after her name. Adding the letters MBA and then Ph.D. became my new goals. Acronyms like these would allow my promiscuous reputation to fade away and make a new, accomplished woman of me.

When I wasn't at school or spending time with my family, I was writing. During my college years, I developed a love for it, and I spent hours typing away words I hoped would reach an editor's desk and the print of a local newspaper.

In full righteous mode, I used my writing voice to take a stand and "educate" those who disagreed with me and explain why they were wrong.

So many things bothered me in those days. When you set your standards as high as I did, what else could I expect? I took to the keyboard, typing 90 wpm (I did do well in high school typing class) to produce as many letters to the editor as I could pump out. In my hoity-toity writing voice, I ensured that I was on the right side of every issue at hand.

In an Oral Communications class, I fell in love with public speaking. I liked the idea of using body language to drive further the points I needed to make. When one of my classmates encouraged me to join Toastmasters, ® I jumped at the opportunity.

After a few months, I built up the courage to tackle a "persuasive" speech. At the time, the right for gay couples to marry was in the headlines often, so I chose this as my topic. I was confident that I could sway anyone to believe same-sex marriage is wrong. I spent hours carefully choosing the right Bible verses and loaded the speech with facts gleaned from my conservative-leaning resources.

My Toastmaster's group met every other Wednesday night at a local steak joint in a side banquet room with a superb wine list. I liked to arrive early and sit at the bar for "me" time which included a few glasses of wine at Happy Hour prices. I sat on a bar stool that faced the entrance door so that I could watch for my fellow Toastmasters to arrive. As they did, I motioned for the bartender to fill me up, and I'd find a seat next to a friendly face.

The night of my anti-same-sex-marriage speech, the group leader handed out the meeting agenda and I was second up. I had practiced the speech in front of my family the night before, took in their feedback, and felt ready to go. Before diving in, I introduced myself, said something funny to relax the crowd, and then began the art of persuasion. I finished before the timed bell rang, sat back down, and waited for my notecards.

After a Toastmaster speech, the audience will provide feedback. It's supposed to be constructive so that we can learn to be better speakers. After the 10 minutes was up (everything has a timer), the notes were collected, handed to me and I tucked them away to read at the bar afterward while enjoying more "me" time with a nightcap.

As I sat sipping a new glass of Cabernet (my favorite red), I was encouraged by the first few notes I read. "Your eye contact was excellent," "You took the right amount of pause before beginning a new thought" and "You were very convincing by adding the report from such and such." One even stated my posture made me look confident. Whew, so far so good, I thought.

Then I read a note from Betsy. She was a lesbian and told me that my speech offended her, and it was mean-spirited. Yikes, I didn't see this coming, as I didn't realize we had a gay person in our group. She schooled me by sharing real life experiences as a gay woman and the pain associated with the very judgment I spouted in my speech.

I don't know if it was the 6+ glasses of wine I drank or the pain in her words, but suddenly I felt uneasy about my speech. Other than close family and friends, it was the first time I experienced a person negatively impacted by my righteous words.

Betsy had succeeded in knocking me off my high-horse. She belittled me into humility. I got to thinking, what if someone had given a speech against teenage sex and the immorality associated with that behavior? How offended would I be? Very offended, I am certain. So why was I sitting in judgment of others?

The whole righteous act that I had gotten so good at was only a front to keep my past a secret. Delving into highly charged controversial issues kept me sidetracked and my mind too busy to deal with my demons.

After my experience with Betsy, I couldn't get Romans 2:1 out of my head, "You, therefore, have no excuse, you who pass judgment on someone else, for at whatever point you judge another, you are condemning yourself, because you who pass judgment do the same thing."

From that time on, I took on the "let's agree to disagree" and the "if I don't have anything nice to say, don't say anything at all" attitude.

My new outlook was helped when my daughter went on a mission trip to Denver,

Colorado before her freshman year of high school. Upon her return, she shared stories that astonished me. Her experience was life-changing.

Of the many stories she told, one stood out the most. It was a homeless man who thanked her for the time she took during the summer to help in his community. He was torn and tattered, but cheerful and full of grace. I thought, "How is this possible?" His only belongings were in a black plastic garbage bag. He didn't have a home, a car, regular meals, regular showers or clean clothes to wear. How did he have such grace?

I felt desperate to experience what she had and was moved to call the church and offer my leadership on the next trip. The next summer, I was on a bus to a coal mining community in West Virginia with four other leaders and 25 teenagers, which included my daughter. My life would never be the same, and West Virginia would not be my last mission trip.

Each trip added a new perspective to my life-view, and it changed my life for the better. The things I once took for granted could bear witness to the most change.

Before mission work, I hated being poor and hated living paycheck to paycheck. However, after West Virginia, I was thankful that I had a paycheck, as most folks in that coal mining community didn't have one. They were dirty and poor; many had no electricity or running water. Three meals a day was a luxury. I was thankful to be on the side of the soup line where I served the guests and not the other way around.

Witnessing those suffering children tore at my heart. I couldn't help but think, what if these were my kids? Hungry, abused, and neglected; desperate for love. No child should live in conditions not even fit for a dog.

Though heartbreaking, there was a significant silver lining. It came from the inevitable transformation in the lives of the teenagers from our church. I witnessed their relationship with Jesus grow and strengthen throughout the mission week, and by the end of the journey, they were changed too.

On one mission trip in the Deep South, our group attended a Baptist Church service with an all-Black congregation. As an entirely white Catholic Church group from the Mid-West, we had no idea what to expect. We are familiar with what can be defined as the most ritualized church service in all organized religion. There isn't much chance of a shake-up at a Catholic Mass. It's too predictable.

That afternoon, it was sweltering hot as we walked through the church doors, praying for air conditioning. There was none. We were led to the front of the church to take our seats. You could tell the church was old by the character of the benches we sat on. We were a large group of about 40 (other missionaries from another State joined), and we had to squeeze close together so that the regular church goers could sit too.

It didn't take long before the smell of perspiration arose in the already stale and still air. Thankfully, the choir started up distracting my sense of smell. There wasn't an organ-led song as we were accustomed to in our church. Not at all. It was loud, joyful and exuberant. They used drums, tambourines, and even a trumpet. In all my years of going to Catholic Mass, there was not one time I could recall clapping during a song of praise.

Awkwardly, our group tried to loosen up as they attempted to sway back and forth and clap their hands like the regulars. If I wasn't a leader at the time, I might have laughed out loud. I almost felt sorry for our teens because they looked so uncomfortable and had no rhythm whatsoever in comparison to the church's members.

As the songs of praise ended, the Pastor began to speak. She was a black woman and needed no microphone to be heard. She was loud and full of vigor. Her words were provocative and bold. She stood right in front of our group and didn't mince words. She called us sinners and said we would not reach Heaven's gate unless we repent and break our hearts open in Jesus name.

She shouted that we had to drop the baggage we were dragging around and leave it, with our pain, at the foot of the cross. Slowly tears began running down my hot and sweaty cheeks. Then as fast as I wiped them, more came. Was she talking to me? How could she know? I looked over at my husband, and he was crying too. Was God using this woman to rescue us from our past? She kept on; she was relentless.

We were invited to come forward, and soon we stood at the foot of the altar, and she kept on. She lowered her voice and said no matter what we've done, regardless of where we have been, Jesus forgives everything. All we had to do to find peace, was to ask for forgiveness and accept it. We can't revisit it or ask for it again when we feel bad. We had to leave it and move on.

With puffy red eyes and a shaky body, I lowered my head and did as she said. As if it happened today, I vividly remember this was the day I finally let go of my past. As the choir chimed in and softly sang Amazing Grace, I knew God spoke to me through this outspoken Pastor. I let go of all the pain associated with my horrendous past: sex addiction, abortions, lies, torment, loneliness, and guilt – they were all as good as gone.

All the shackles and chains which bound me for too many years were finally set free. As the Pastor closed the service, she said, "From this moment on, you are not who you used to be. We put our failures in the hands of Jesus, and we are unequivocally redeemed." And with that, I walked out of that church a brand new child of Christ.

PART TWO

UNABRIDGED

CHAPTER THREE

Shenanigans

One of my earliest childhood memories is of my mom crying and speed-walking all around our modest home in a rural Wisconsin township. It was nightfall in springtime in 1972. Her weeping turned into yelling. "No! No! No! Not now," she bellowed. I was frightened and couldn't move.

As best as I can remember, I had never seen her cry like that, or ever. She was racing from cupboard to dresser, swinging doors open and pulling drawers out. She was searching for something that was not there anymore. Dad's things were gone. They were gone because he left us. I was five years old.

Earlier in the day, we celebrated my older sister's sixth birthday. It seemed that all of my sister's first-grade classmates were in our backyard. I was in the thick of it, joining in and having a blast. We played ring-around-the-rosy and pin-the-tail on the donkey. We bobbed for apples, wore party hats, and sounded horns. We were carefree and played the part of five and six-year-olds to a tee. Mom was none the wiser that inside the house, dad was packing his things and moving out.

Our family included my mom and dad, my older brother by two years, my older sister by one year and a younger sister by two years. For all I've learned over the years, we were a typical all-American family. Mom's job was traditional; she took care of us kids, cleaned the house, and made meals. Dad earned money.

When he walked out of our lives, he took mom's best friend, Paula with him. It is not for lack of effort, I never fully grasped why he left. For years, I tried to understand. I guess some things are never meant to be figured out. Boy, his departure sure messed up our lives.

My parents' divorced soon after that dreadful night. My mom became broken-hearted and sad. Who wouldn't be? One afternoon you are celebrating your daughter's sixth birthday, and hours later you find out that your husband had a secret life.

Thankfully, my grandparents stepped in and rearranged their lives to fit us in. They lived on the South Side of Milwaukee. Mostly raised in the city, they were devout Catholics and wonderful people in their own ways. How they came to be as a couple is unique. My dad's dad married my mom's mom.

When my mom was 14 years old, her biological father died from cancer, and when dad was a young man serving in the Navy, his mom died from alcoholism. After dad and mom dated for a while, they played cupid, and the result was marriage. My grandparents got married not too long after my parents wedded.

Understandably, my parent's divorce brought about side swipes from grandmother. She unapologetically bashed my dad and branded him a monster. It didn't matter that we heard every cut-down. She seemed not to care that grandpa was in earshot of her remarks either. My dad broke my mom's heart, and grandma was pissed off. As much as she loathed him, she hated his new wife even more and never let us kids forget how she despised Paula.

Living with my grandparents was less than ideal. However, what choice did we have? My mom had to figure out how to be a single parent for four small children. She needed a plan and time to grieve the loss of a life that would never come to be with dad.

Mom didn't go to college, but she has always had an incredible work ethic. She sharpened this during her adolescent years after her father passed away. Being the second oldest of nine children, she was expected to work to help put food on the table. She went from school, straight to the church rectory and home to help with chores.

Mom ended up getting a job at a bakery, and in no time she was promoted to a management position. She worked long hours, sometimes 12-

hour shifts. Soon we were living on our own and made a new start.

Dad wasn't a complete monster; he did pay child support. However, he only paid the minimum amount the court ordered and nothing more. From there his commitment to us kids only extended to visits twice a year. One week in the summer and a week over Christmas break.

He didn't live nearby; dad lived up north about three hours away. He would drive to Milwaukee to pick us up, and we'd drive to what he called God's country. We always had fun when we visited dad. In the winter, we bar-hopped on snowmobiles and in the summer, we floated on his pontoon boat from sunrise to sunset. I didn't much like Paula, though.

Perhaps this was because of the deep-rooted abhorrence planted by grandma. On the other hand, maybe it was because she wasn't my real mom and I didn't like seeing her affectionate with dad. Or perhaps, it was because she had "stolen" dad from us. Whatever the reason, it would take many moons before my heart would change.

After the second grade, mom transferred us kids to a Catholic grade school. It was structured and strict. Not only did I go to church every Sunday, but I also went during the school week with my classmates. The Parish Priest taught Religion class, and most of my teachers were nuns.

By today's standards, I am sure I had ADHD. I had zero focus and never could sit still. My mind was always racing on anything other than the task at hand. I adored gym class and recess because I could get crazy without getting into trouble. But in the classroom, I struggled and often got scolded.

My favorite teacher at that school was Mrs. Grum in third grade. She reminded me of my grandmother when my grandmother was in a good mood. She was chubby and jolly. Her classroom had boatloads of children's books she read with zeal and animation during story times.

As I got comfortable in my new surroundings, I began to develop a wild streak which was fueled by a new friendship I made. Marie, a funny girl who showcased dimples when she laughed quickly became my best friend. My hair was long and auburn, hers was short and blonde. My skin was olive, and hers light. We looked opposite but shared the same twisted humor. We began to establish rabble-rouser reputations.

As was common in a Catholic school in those days, the principal was a nun. She was strict and mean, and didn't tolerate misbehavior. Sister John Fischer was a stocky woman with dark-rimmed glasses and pale skin. She wore a black and white habit every day, including a tunic and flat, dull black shoes. She also wore the same expression on her face most of the time; stoic.

Marie and I vowed that Sister John Fischer was not going to ruin the fun we planned to get away with during the school year. The girl's locker room was in the basement of the school, and her office was on the second floor. A back stairway led to her room from the basement. The principal's desk faced the wall, so when you entered her office, her back was against you.

One afternoon after volleyball practice, Marie and I snuck up the stairs with a soaked paper towel in hand and threw it hard over her head so that it would stick to the wall above her. As soon as we witnessed she was startled, we raced back down the stairs, barely able to hold in our giggling. The next day when we passed her office doorway and spotted the stain from the wet paper towel on the wall, we would giggle all over again.

During recess, you'd find Marie and me throwing small stones at the heads of the boys tossing a football around. When our aim was just right, we looked the other way, claiming innocence, all the while busting a gut from laughing so hard.

In the warm months, we'd gather up ants into an envelope brought from home and then drop them on the head of a classmate during the next class period. We had a handful of victims we picked on the most, that day was JoAnn. As the ants weaved around her hair, she became antsy (pun intended), red faced, and embarrassed when the little black critters fell onto her desk. We tried our best not to laugh out loud.

My student evaluations proved that I was spending more time as an agitator than almost anything else. My fifth grade teacher, Sr. Marie Dorothy Murphy noted, "I did not help to create a pleasant learning experience." In sixth grade, the only classes I was "satisfactory" in were spelling, art, and writing. In all my other classes, I failed, including Religion class (this, of course, being at a parochial school.)

Even outside of school, Marie and I hunted for victims to satisfy our demented sense of humor. We'd find luck at the mall by going to the second floor to find unsuspecting targets below, preferably bald headed men. We were always pleasantly surprised of how many cue balls were in the mall. In a sling-shot speed, we'd fire anything that could bounce off and leave a mark of evidence. Depending on the time of year, chestnuts or candy raisins were our weapons of choice.

On the weekends, Marie and I hung out at Square Park. It must have gotten its name because the entire block was *the park*. It had the standard playground equipment, a community swimming pool, and a recreation building where volunteers helped the kiddos in the neighborhood with crafts during the summer.

We hung out mostly on the playground. Somehow we cajoled kids to go down the giant slide on their little riding toys. We double-dog-dared them and found not too many could resist such a provocation. Square Park had one of the tallest slides I knew about, and this was essential for the speed factor. The smooth metal was also critical. Between the hot metal and sky high height, the kids had no chance to make it down without flying uncontrollably into the sand. We roared with laughter just on the facial expressions alone.

In fourth grade, my mouth got taped shut by my teacher, Ms. Sood. She had warned me many times to shut-up, but to no avail. She grabbed duct tape from her old wooden desk and smothered it over my mouth, right in front of the other students. As they snickered, I panicked because I was a mouth breather at the time. I was finding it hard to breathe, and I was utterly humiliated.

Fortunately, that was my last class of the day. Once the bell rang, I tore off the tape and took some skin with it. I skipped volleyball practice and raced home. There I examined my face in the mirror. I looked like a damn clown with wide red lips. I wasn't sure how I was going to explain this to my mom.

When mom got home from work, she asked what happened. I decided honesty was the best policy in this situation and I told her my teacher taped my mouth shut because I wouldn't stop talking. She flew off the handle, picked up the phone, dialed the convent and demanded to speak with Sister John Fischer.

My mom's words were sharp and clear. This teacher was to be nowhere near me ever again. With that, she got a pink slip. It was the first time I ever witnessed my mom get angry and defensive of me. I felt like a baby cub being protected by mama bear.

The duck-tape incident brought the saying, what comes around, goes around to my mind. I was embarrassed to show my Ronald McDonald look-a-like face at school the next day and experienced what it felt like to be on the receiving end of humiliation.

I wish I could say I learned my lesson and never got into trouble after that, but I'd be lying. I continued to be a hellion and got into more trouble as the years went on. Though I never got any more teachers fired.

As I reached the end of my eighth-grade year, I started getting excited about high school. I would be going to the very same one that mom went to back in the 1950s, and where my older sister, Kelly, was already attending. No more nuns, priests, rules, and Religion class. And Marie was going there too.

CHAPTER FOUR

40 Miles West

Then my life went through another major re-write. Like nine years earlier, we'd have a new home and a new city to get to know.

Mom met a recently divorced man named Allan while at a birthday party for her and her twin sister. Allan worked with mom's twin sister at a local cannery plant.

He owned a house in a small city about forty miles West of Milwaukee and had full custody of his two sons. My aunt hosted the party in a neighboring city from where my life began. As cliché as it may be, they fell in love at first sight.

My memory is blurry of any courtship mom and Allan had. However, I remember when I first met his sons. The older boy was eleven years old, and his younger brother was nine. I was amused with their small-town mentality as we wandered around the neighborhood when they would visit us in Milwaukee.

With boombox in hand, listening to "Another One Bites the Dust" by Queen, my older sister and I were their big city tour guides. The tour consisted of walking to Mitchell Street, which at the time, was a happening place. If ever you wanted to buy a wedding dress, Mitchell Street was the place to go. You'd find me, as well as thousands of other girls, peering through the storefront windows over time at the glamorous dresses and wondered if we'd be so lucky to wear one someday.

We never did any shopping on Mitchell Street. We just strolled around and got to know one another. When we were given money from our parents, which was rare, we'd go to the candy store. There we could buy candy raisins and

Swedish fish for a penny a piece. We'd always end at Square Park, right around the block from my house.

By the end of our excursions, it was dark out, and we were usually the only ones around. You'd be able to see the most sky sitting on the swings, as there were no tall buildings for an entire block radius.

As young kids sometimes do, we tried to be show-offs and act cool. From naming the stars in the sky to the television shows we were allowed to watch, we enjoyed learning more about each other. Their eyes popped when I told them we watched "Three's Company" with my mom on Wednesday nights. They weren't allowed to watch that show, and I felt "one-up" on them.

Never once did we consider that our parents would be anything other than two people dating, at least we never talked about it. I for one did not realize their embraces and kisses were a preamble to marriage. My young and immature 13-year-old mind prevented me from seeing the big picture and how my life could be turned upside down relatively soon.

No matter how many times I search my memory, I cannot recall the moment when I learned they were getting married and that we would be moving 40 miles west to a city, less than a quarter the size of Milwaukee. Various therapists have told me over the years that people tend to bury traumatic events so deep they can never be retrieved.

Some would argue that your mom getting married and finding happiness after being treated like yesterday's garbage by your dad is hardly a traumatic event. However, I would argue back that leaving my home and all of my friends was upsetting, especially for a 13-year-old. Not being able to go to high school with your best friend sucked.

Well, at least my mom was still planning on throwing my eighth-grade graduation party before we moved. I had looked forward to my party since my brother had his own party two years earlier and my sister, one year ago. As customary in parochial grade schools, one has a celebratory party after graduation Mass. Mom threw the party in our backyard and invited all my aunts, uncles, grandparents, and cousins. Except for a few who lived out of state, most of them came, including my "soon-to-be-new" family.

There are two things I remember most about that party. First, the brand new ten-speed bicycle I got. It was shiny blue, and it was the first bike I had ever owned. Whenever I wanted to bicycle, I'd borrow one from Marie. Besides a car accident I'd experience later in life, the only other painful incident I had was on one of Marie's bikes. At least an accident worthy of the few scars I still have today.

One afternoon, Marie and I were biking carefree all over the South Side. We didn't have a destination; we only wanted to spin wheels. Marie warned me that her dad had tightened the break lines of all their bikes and cautioned me to tap them, instead of squeezing them in when I needed to stop.

We were obsessed with popping tar bubbles, and it was a hot summer day. For every street we came upon with newly poured blacktop, we'd stop to see if we could find any. We came upon a street that was half-way done. One side was glazing black, and the other faded gray with cracks and small stones. This street was on a hill, and we were heading down it fast but planned to stop at the bottom for some bubble popping.

Unfortunately, a kickball got in the way. Trying to avoid it would force me over to the new side of the street and would ruin the bike wheels I was riding on. Instead, I instinctively squeezed the breaks, forgetting what Marie warned and flipped in the air and into the hard gravel on the old side of the street.

I came down hard and was amazed that I did not break any bones. I did break the bike though, and I felt awful about it. It was a tangled mess, which meant I couldn't get back on it and ride it home. I was a mess too. The right side of my body was the worst; my cheek bone was gouged with little pebbles embedded in the skin, as well as my elbow, knee, and foot – all of the prominent parts of my body that took a beating upon impact.

Besides my birth and getting my tonsils out, I didn't visit hospitals. It wasn't part of my childhood. I desired to keep it that way. Trying to be tough and avoid an ER visit, I wobbled the bike and myself home with Marie patiently walking next to me with her bike. I kept telling her I was sorry for destroying the bike and she kept telling me I should be more worried about me.

When I got home, I looked in the mirror and was horrified. I understood what Marie meant! My face looked like it got hauled through a stone pit with sharp spiky rocks. The cuts were small but significant enough for blood to emerge and make me look like a bleeding pin cushion. That was my last bike excursion with Marie, ever.

As I looked at my brand-new bike, I sadly thought those wheels would never roll in and around the streets which had become a part of me over the last nine years. No more tar bubble pursuits and carefree rides around the city with my best friend. For the first time in my recent memory, I was sad.

The second memory about that day were the words told to me by one of my uncles. His words, or a variance of, are likely shared with other grade school graduates and perhaps high school and college students as well. I'm certain he was only being nice and could not have known that years later his words would resurface at a pivotal time in my life.

Racing through the front door to catch up with my cousins, an uncle stopped me on the front porch. Two other uncles were in a deep conversation with Pabst Blue Ribbon beer bottles in hand. The weather was perfect that day, temps in the 70s with a steady sun. My uncle stopped me right before descending the steps, and at the part of the porch with no sun protection.

As he looked at me, he squinted his eyes from the sun and remarked that I was a special young lady. For a second I felt embarrassed and thought he might be drunk. It wouldn't be unheard of, as my family is of the drinking kind. He seemed sober enough as he went on to tell me that one day I would help change this world for the better.

Hmmm. At age 13, I wasn't sure what my uncle meant; but his words were warm and caring, and I said, "Thank you," and gave him a hug.

Later in the evening, I jotted down the highlights of this special day in my diary. I wrote in quotations, "I will change the world for the better someday because I am special." Then with a heavy heart, I shut the book, locked it with its tiny key, and placed it in a box of things which would soon get loaded onto a moving truck.

In August of 1981, mom married Allan, now my step-dad. She wore a lovely linen colored dress that brushed the floor and a hat decorated with lace. Allan was handsome in a sharp black suit, and all of us kids wore new outfits bought just for the occasion. They wedded in a small chapel, not our church. Family and friends from his side and ours sat on their respective sides of the isle.

My grandpa walked mom to the archway adorned with cheesy fake flowers where Allan stood next to the officiant. It was stuffy, and I fidgeted in my seat wondering when we could get out of that hot box. After a couple of stern glances from an aunt, I folded my hands on my lap and patiently waited for the "I do" words and the kiss.

One of my sisters was sniffling next to me. I couldn't tell if her tears were happy ones, or sad. If she felt like I did, they were sad. Following my graduation party, I had nothing but a gloomy outlook. And this day sealed the deal for me. We were moving away from our life in Milwaukee and into the unknown. I was along just for the ride, and my feelings about it didn't matter.

A reception followed which would include food, dancing, and alcohol. It was loud and bustling. We kids were quarantined to a table next to our parents. We didn't see much of them that day, but every time my eyes found mom, she had a smile from ear to ear. It seemed as if everyone was having a grand time; I even had fun watching the adults act silly on the dance floor. I was amused by a few of my relatives, as I had never seen them that crazy and wild. I didn't realize at the time that it was likely alcohol induced.

After enjoying the adults' spectacle, I peered over at my new stepbrother, Shawn. He was cute with his curly brown hair and a big smile, and he was laughing about something along with my siblings. For a moment, I felt an odd attraction to him and quickly brushed it away. It was late, I was tired, and it had been a long day. Nothing I was feeling at the moment meant anything, I reasoned. He was my new stepbrother, after all.

Shortly after the wedding, we moved west. Allan's house sat on a dead-end street in a modest neighborhood. I had to share a bedroom with my sisters again, but this time in a much (MUCH) smaller room. It was so small that we had to buy a bunk bed equipped with a trundle and tuck it away every morning so that we could move around in the daylight.

The house had a total of two bedrooms, one bathroom, a separate dining room, living room, and small kitchen. My "new" step-grandpa was a master carpenter, and he helped to remodel half of the unfinished basement into a LARGE bedroom for the boys. One whole half of the basement became their bedroom, while the other half was the laundry room which housed the furnace and miscellaneous storage.

So the boys got triple the size of the girls' bedroom. How was this fair? Why didn't we buy a bigger house? Things weren't starting out well, at least in my opinion. But I already had a chip on my shoulder, so almost anything would add to my crappy outlook.

Meanwhile, the attraction I felt for Shawn on our parents' wedding night kept on. I could see and feel he was attracted to me as well and soon we were doing inappropriate things with each other in secret. We started sneaking around on a regular basis, and it seemed our parents and siblings were oblivious to what was happening.

As this storm was brewing, there was a lot of tension at home, and everyone was feeling the strain of having to deal with the new dynamics of a blended family. The best way I dealt with it was to escape with Shawn. This flight would eventually lead to a catastrophic storm with damaging effects that lasted for years.

CHAPTER FIVE

Dirty Little Secret

Anyone who knew me intimately in the early 1980s would likely tell you I was off-balance, that something was amiss with me. I wore a lot of makeup and obsessed with my hair and body. Sounds like any teenage girl, past, and present, right? However, I had an added element not so unique to a 14-year-old. I was "addicted" to sex.

Not addicted to sex with anyone, I was addicted to sex with my 12-year-old stepbrother. We had sex as often as we could and wherever we could get away with not getting caught. It was common for me to sneak into the boys' bedroom in the middle of the night and climb into bed with Shawn. Never mind both of our brothers were only a few feet away; we were as quiet as we could be.

During the daylight, when we thought no one was watching, we'd slip into the garage, the laundry room, or the bathroom. The place was irrelevant; what was crucial was never being seen, heard, or suspected. We needed the physical act of having sex because we had become addicts, plain and simple.

Speaking for myself, I needed an escape from the blended mess I thought my family had become. Being with Shawn helped me if only in brief spurts of time, to put aside the bitterness I was harboring from being ripped away from Milwaukee. I felt trapped in a so-called "chapter of my life," one of which I was not the author and had no control.

As with most addictions, reckless and crazy behaviors are par for the course. Clarity and proper judgment cannot bear witness in an addict's life. Sex addiction is no different. An addict will lie, cheat, and steal to get a fix. For me, the first one, lying, would lead to my eventual fall.

One definition of reckless is: "Heedless of danger or the consequences of one's actions; rash or impetuous."[1] It's as though this word existed because of people like me and Shawn who had sex without protection when they don't wish to get pregnant. Or worse, not caring if they did. As crazy as it sounds, this is how we conducted our secret sex life.

We were extremely reckless never using any birth control. We never even talked about it or surmised what would happen if I ever did get pregnant. It was simply never a voiced thought or concern. And why should it be? I was never

---

[1]

Https://en.oxforddictionaires.com/definition/reckless. (n.d.). Retrieved March 3, 2017.

taught the birds and the bees, per say. I didn't know much about anything when it came to the baby making parts of my body.

For more than two years we had unprotected sex, which gave us a false confidence of not suffering any consequences. As misguided as it is, we felt luck was on our side.

That was until the summer of 1983. My period didn't come on time, and it always came on time. At least I was aware that if a girl has sex and she does not get her period, she could be pregnant. Unfortunately, I never connected the possibility of such a dramatic outcome to my secret sex life.

After a couple of weeks of silent panic, I finally told Shawn I thought I was pregnant and we had to figure out what to do about our *situation*. Of all the options, telling our parents was not one of them. Telling anyone was not an option. So we did what we did best, we lied. And not a small lie, a whopper of one that truthfully contained all the bells and whistles of two very disturbed teenagers, desperately needing professional help.

That summer, I had been babysitting for Aunt Lynn and Uncle Ryan in a neighboring city on the weekends. Their house is where we decided to take care of our *situation*. The plan was irrational, delusional, and maybe even criminal.

The idea was to fake that I was raped and to pretend a man lurking in the wooded area of my aunt and uncle's property lunged out and forced himself on me. This scheme would be a tough sell, as the neighborhood and even the city had zero crime. But I had no choice; I had to convince them I was a victim of a horrific crime.

After they had left for the night, I set the scene and played my part. I messed my hair, smudged my make-up and tore my clothes. Sadly, playing the part was easy for me. Maybe it was my raging hormones from being pregnant or the desperation I felt for my situation; whatever the case, I pulled it off. I even mustered some genuine tears for when the police arrived.

It's hard to recall all that happened after the police came to the house. I do remember being taken to the hospital and examined. It was one of

those creepy exams you see on Law & Order
SVU, where the nurse combs through your hair
and body searching for any evidence of the
perpetrator.

Thankfully, Shawn and I were not intimate for
a few days. We never thought that any evidence
of him on or in my body would have derailed the
plan. A doctor finished the exam and reported
she could not find any semen or other evidence
which could be used to identify a rapist. (Of
course, they didn't)

An officer asked if I was up to coming to the
police station to look at mugshots. Crap, this was
getting more serious, I thought. If I said no, I felt
I could raise suspicion. So I said, sure. I vaguely
remember turning the pages, searching for a man
that did not exist.

After paging through a few books, I said I was
tired and wanted to go home. The officer sitting
with me nodded in agreement and motioned for
my family. He assured them that they would do
all they could to find the man responsible for my
rape.

In life, it sometimes takes years to gain a
proper perspective to poor decisions you've made

and the impact they have on others. This particular event is one of those.

There were so many other choices we could have made. The most obvious choice, the truth, had it been told, would have been difficult but could have saved heartache and pain for many people involved. Perhaps it could have set in motion the necessary actions and conditions which may have prevented even more heartache that was yet to come to Shawn and me.

Uncle Ryan blamed himself for my attack because he was not home to prevent it. It was the first time I ever saw one of my uncles cry. Moreover, years later I would learn the oldest cousin I babysat feared her neighborhood for many moons after that night. These are only the consequences I am aware of.

A few weeks later, mom and I sat in the doctor's office and received official confirmation that I was indeed pregnant.

The date was September 23, 1983; it was my 16th birthday. I sat on the table while mom sat on a chair in the exam room. Casually the doctor explained our choices. Have the baby and keep it, have the baby and give it up for adoption, or have an abortion.

The choice was clear, made evident by my theatrics. After all, who would want to give birth to a baby conceived by rape? The doctor handed my mom information about a Planned Parenthood clinic in Milwaukee, and we headed for home.

There wasn't much to say on the walk back. I could not and would not confess to Shawn being the father of my baby. How would I approach such a conversation anyway? Would I say, "Oh, by the way, I'm the biggest liar in the world... I wasn't raped, and furthermore, I've been having sex with Shawn since we moved into their house?"

In my mind, the truth was impossible, and I had to take what was coming and accept it as the only viable solution.

Shawn and I had an understanding that I was on my own in this big fat lie. The less he was involved, the better chance we had of getting away with it and getting back to our secret sex. I wanted to resume where we left off before I thought I was pregnant. Now more than ever, I needed an escape.

My pregnancy ended a few days following my 16th birthday. Instead of celebrating a "sweet" sixteenth; I was destroying a life. That birthday would forever be marked as a sad and shameful one. Subsequent birthdays would mean nothing to me; I hated when the family tried to make a big deal of them every year after.

Like the blind leading the blind, mom and I had no idea what to expect when we arrived at Planned Parenthood on a brisk, sunny morning. One of my mom's friends, Tammy, drove us and as we entered the building, the sun went away. The windows inside were tinted and dark. I think the outside windows had a mirrored effect so that no one could see inside. It was an eerie and cold place.

When we reached the reception desk, a young woman in her early 20s peered up and asked for a patient name. She had zero personality and no smile as she used her highlighter pen to mark me as arrived. Then she directed us to take a seat.

There weren't many open chairs in the waiting area; it was almost full of women and men. They all seemed to have the same look we must have had; bewilderment. I sat and scanned my surroundings. This place was unlike the doctor's office I was just at days earlier. There were no friendly paintings on the walls, no greenery on the tables, no magazines, and no television. There was nothing to distract me from the fear I began to feel.

A woman standing in a doorway across the room called my name. Like the receptionist, she had no personality either. She wore scrubs, and her hair was pulled back in a tight bun. Her eyes were dull, reminiscent of someone who was depressed and sad.

She held the door open and motioned for me to step through. As I did, I knew there was no turning back. My lies perpetrated the end of my pregnancy, and I only had myself to blame. Soon Shawn's baby would be gone.

The nurse led me to a procedure room, shut the door, and told me to take off my clothes. She placed a gown on the table and gestured that I needed to put it on. She didn't give me any privacy as she continued to organize instruments on a metal tray.

There was no small talk while we waited for the doctor. I was freezing cold and shivering as I sat on the table trying to cover my exposed skin with the short knee-high gown I was given. The nurse never offered me a blanket.

Once the doctor entered the room, he glanced at my chart and then instructed me to lie back and scoot to the end of the table so that he could put my legs in stirrups. He never introduced himself to me, and he never asked if I had any questions or concerns about the procedure.

Without further ado, he took what looked like a hand-held vacuum, turned on a switch, and sucked my baby right out of my body.

As quickly as he had entered the room, he was gone. The nurse was left to clean the mess, both on me and on the silver tray where the vacuum tube sat. As she wiped things with a rag and some stinky solution from a spray bottle, she told me to get dressed. Then she walked me back to the waiting room.

As I searched for my mom, I wished I was a little girl again. I wanted to run into her arms and have her hold me and tell me everything was going to be alright. But I couldn't, I had to be brave and not show any emotion. Mom needed to believe I was relieved that I no longer had a rapist's baby inside of me.

If only I could confess and tell mom all I was feeling. Maybe she wouldn't be mad at me for lying. Perhaps she would send me to talk to someone who could help me overcome the immense sorrow that crept into my soul the moment the doctor shut off that machine.

But I couldn't bring myself to tell her the truth. It was too late. As mom and Tammy chit-chatted in the front seat, I kept quiet in the backseat for the entire drive home. I had nothing to say because I couldn't put into words the sadness I was feeling.

CHAPTER SIX

Darn Fate

A day before my abortion, someone told me, "It'll be good to get back to a normal life afterward." What is normal? One dictionary defines normal as "conforming to a standard; usual, typical, or expected."[2] At age sixteen, nothing about my life for years before or after would fit into that definition.

---

[2] Https://en.oxforddictionaries.com/definition/normal. (n.d.). Retrieved April 10, 2017.

Before moving west, my life seemed like every other kid I knew at the time. I might have been a goof at school and ran a bit wild with Marie, but I was a typical adolescent.

There is no explanation for why I ran amuck and deviated from normal behavior once my mom got married. I cannot pinpoint a specific date and time when I went from a virgin at age fourteen to a sex addict. I didn't write about it in my diary or put it on a calendar. It just evolved over a short period of time.

Sex was never a thought before the move westward. There was never a reason to talk about it, and it didn't cross my mind at the Catholic grade school I attended, which is expected at such a young age. It certainly was not a topic at home with my family.

The only time sex may have been brought up, was likely in Religion class when we had been told that our bodies must remain pure until our wedding day. I am sure I accepted that premise, all the while giggling about the word *sex* being said out loud by our Priest.

It's as though all the Catholic teachings that had been instilled in me were forgotten and left in a box back in Milwaukee. Somehow those virtues never made it onto the moving truck. Without them in my new life, my conscience stopped working properly. Deep down I knew right from wrong, but I didn't care.

This made it easy to fall back into my secret sex life with Shawn shortly after my abortion. I neatly filed my abortion into a compartment in my head, along with all the sadness, shame, and guilt and placed a heavy duty lock on it. I could not allow it to interfere with the escape my body craved with Shawn.

We tried to be more careful from that point; Shawn pulled out just in time. This became our new birth control method, and soon enough, it would fail.

It's hard to remember the exact time when our parents became suspicious of us, but when they did, chances of being alone diminished drastically, almost entirely. Like any addict, it's hard to quit cold turkey, and we were being forced to give up a habit without anything to replace it.

There was no support group to turn to, and no addiction counseling offered. Why would there be? Our parents had no clue of how extensive our secret lives together had become. And we were not about to divulge any of it.

As we got more desperate to be alone, we made stupid missteps. One afternoon, we did not check to see if anyone was upstairs as we snuck out to the garage. We knew no one was in the kitchen and living room; we checked those places. However, our window of opportunity was tiny, so we didn't take the time to check elsewhere. Just as we were zipping up our jeans, my mom opened the garage door.

A few days later, I was sent to live with Aunt Lynn and Uncle Ryan for the last semester of my junior year. Mom didn't actually see us having sex, but she surmised something had taken place by the look of surprise we couldn't hide on our faces.

As I sat on the guest bed at my aunt and uncle's place, I couldn't believe that I was kicked out of my home. Banished from it. Banished from Shawn. I wanted to die.

Why was I being punished? Why only me? Why didn't Shawn have to move away? These unasked questions swam around my head for a while as I sat feeling sorry for myself. I even invited God to my pity party by asking Him, "Why are you doing this to me, how much more suffering are you going to make me go through?"

As I invoked God in my mess, I couldn't recall the last time I went to church or even spent time with Him in prayer. Was the absence of this why my life was so broken? I harkened back to Milwaukee and remembered how the church was such a big part of my life. Now we only went on Holidays like Christmas and Easter. I used to say prayers daily, and now I said none.

A few boxes of my things sat near the closet I would use for my temporary stay. I went to the box I knew my diary was in and pulled it out. My mom gave me the diary when I turned nine years old. It was small with a Holly Hobbie looking girl on the cover and a strap on the back that hooked around to fasten at the front. It came with a tiny key so that I could lock away my secret words from snooping sisters.

The last time I had opened that diary was the night following my eighth-grade graduation party. As I re-read some of the pages, I felt sad. My life was so simple then, and I missed those days more than ever. My uncle's words seemed like a joke now; I couldn't fathom how on earth I would make the world a better place with the mess I was making with my life.

I wanted to add new entries filled with as much silliness as my previous ones, but I wrote nothing. Only sadness lived in my heart, and I didn't want to darken my diary with gloom and doom. I shut the book and tossed it back in the box.

As soon as the school year ended, I was allowed to move back home. Shawn was sent to live with his grandparents in a neighboring town for the summer. Much like when a baby first learns to crawl, and the parents are extra vigilant in making sure she doesn't come upon anything dangerous, all eyes watched Shawn and me with the same zeal.

Then in a move that made me more miserable, Shawn was sent to live with Sandra, his mom, in Milwaukee for the next school year. I thought it was outrageous, and I vowed to find a way to outsmart them and be alone with Shawn again.

My senior year of high school should have been an exciting time for me. As my friends were busy making college plans, I was finding a way to visit Shawn in secret. Thankfully, I had a job and began squirreling money away so that I could buy a bus ticket to Milwaukee.

When I had enough saved, Shawn and I put a new plan into action. He lied and told his mom he was sick in the morning and she fell for it, allowing him to stay home from school. I pretended to go to school, but then boarded a Greyhound bus at around the same time that my first class bell would be ringing.

Finally, I thought, as he held open the door to let me in, we were alone. He had the blinds closed in every room; being a cloudy morning, it felt like nighttime as we made our way to the bedroom.

We were too immature to make small talk, and it seemed foreign that he would ask how the bus ride was, or that I would inquire how he liked living with his mom. We didn't care - we had only one thing on our mind, and we didn't waste time talking about anything.

Saying goodbye sucked. I didn't want to raise any suspicion, so I left early to catch the 2:05 pm Greyhound bus back home. If my timing were right, I'd walk through the front door at about the same time as any other day after school.

As I plopped down on the blue cushioned bus seat, I couldn't shake an uneasy feeling. Maybe it was guilt associated with deceiving my mom again? Skipping school? Taking a crazy chance of getting caught? Having sex with Shawn again, unprotected? I couldn't put my finger on why.

Instead, I forced my mind to the last few hours of my life. A grin like that of the Grinch covered my face as I thought about how the plan unfolded perfectly. And they thought they could keep us apart; nice try on their part. But in the end, we had a will and a way to make it work.

When I got home, no one looked at me funny, in fact, as usual, my family ignored me. Whew, we got away with it, I thought. No one was the wiser of our rendezvous, so I proceeded as I usually did when I got home from school. I did my homework, ate supper, helped with the dishes, took a bath and went to bed. And of course, I thought about Shawn and the fun we had earlier in the day.

The next day, I still had an uneasy feeling, and it lingered for weeks. My period was late, and it was never late. So on my way home from school one afternoon, I stopped and bought a pregnancy test. When I got home, I went straight to the bathroom, shut the door and locked it.

This was my first home pregnancy test, so I carefully read the instructions. It said it would take 20 minutes to get the result. A clear stick would mean I wasn't pregnant; a colored one meant I was. So for 20 minutes, I paced back and forth in the small bathroom hoping no one would knock on the door.

After 20 minutes, I sat on the toilet and peered at the stick. I felt my face drain color as the stick gained it. I was pregnant. I was pregnant again. We tempted fate again, and as fate would have it, fate won.

After sitting there for what seemed like forever, one of my sisters knocked on the door. I panicked and placed the test under some empty toilet paper rolls in the garbage to hide it. I went to the bedroom and sat on the edge of my bed. I had no idea how I was going to get out of this pregnancy. No one would believe a trumped-up story like before. I was too scared to think straight.

As luck would have it, mom emptied the garbage from the bathroom right after my sister was done doing her business, and she found the pregnancy test. By then, both my sisters were on their beds as well, as was typical after school before suppertime.

When mom asked us girls about the test, we all denied it as ours. My sisters looked horrified even to be asked; whereas I looked guilty as my face became flushed. I can't remember if my sister's stayed to hear my confession or not, and I cannot even recall the exact words I said. But I did confirm I was the one that bought the pregnancy test.

From there, I quickly came up with a new lie. It was nowhere near the whopper size lie from last summer, but it was all I could come up with lickety-split. I told my mom that a boy I had been dating got me pregnant, and his name is Jeff.

When she asked what his last name was, I refused to tell her and said I would not get him into trouble. That was code for; I would not be getting Shawn into trouble.

Much of that time is foggy; I don't remember much. But after several weeks of hand-wringing, mom had reached the end of her rope with me. Once again I was exiled from my home and found myself unpacking a few boxes of my things in one of my dad's guest bedrooms up north. It was my dad's turn to deal with me. By this time, I was more than a couple of months pregnant.

One cold and rainy morning, we set out to the city of Appleton to end my second pregnancy. I was seventeen years old. As we approached the building, I suddenly felt panic rise in my throat. The compartment in my head where I had locked away my last abortion opened wide, and with it, a flood of memories. I grabbed my dad's arm and said I could not go through the doors. He said it was not up for debate.

As we entered the building, déjà vu surrounded me. I knew we were in a different city than before, but everything inside those walls seemed the same. There were no friendly paintings hung, no television or magazines to flip through, no friendly faces, including the receptionist again. This one too had no personality, and after she had highlighted my name on her patient list, she told us to take a seat. Same as before.

As we sat in the waiting room, the silence was deafening. Fear overcame me as I waited for my name. My dad had to nudge me when it was called. I slowly walked over to the woman that called for me. When I reached the doorway where she stood, she seemed agitated that it took so long for me to get to her.

She didn't tell me her name, so I nicknamed her Nurse Ratchet in my head. Her eyes were dull and drab, and she motioned for me to follow her to the procedure room. The workers in that place looked like the living dead; they had lifeless expressions on their faces as they went about their business.

Nurse Ratchet was no different. Once we were inside the procedure room, she handed me a gown and told me to change into it. I froze, as I knew by following her directive, what the next step would be. Agitated again, she clapped her hands to dismiss my trance and repeated her instruction to change into the gown. I quickly did as she said.

Having already lived this nightmare before, I was not surprised when the doctor entered the room without any introductions. He didn't ask if I had any questions or concerns, he briefly read through my chart and instructed me to scoot down, and then he put my feet in the stirrups.

I never felt as alone as when he began the procedure. He was not gentle; he pulled and scrapped inside me; all the while tears were running down the sides of my face.

At last, he put what he removed from my uterus on a silver tray next to Nurse Ratchet. Then for good measure, he took that same vacuum-like instrument used the year before and sucked out whatever else he thought he had to get. With that, he stood and left, as heartless as the doctor before.

My eyes darted to the silver tray and the contents that looked like a tiny human being. Though distorted, I could make out a leg and an arm. Nurse Ratchet caught this and quickly took the tray to a side room. As she was leaving, she told me to get dressed.

My God, what had I done? I couldn't move, I couldn't get dressed. When she returned from the side room, she was agitated once more that I hadn't moved. My stare pierced her as I asked if that was a *developed* baby she took away. Coldly, she replied I should not have seen what I did. But I did, and it sure looked like a baby, not just a mass of tissue, as I was lead to believe.

My dead baby's image would be hard coded in my memory and would haunt me from that day forward.

On the ride home, I sat silent and stared out through the window, just like the year before. I was so numb and despondent that I wouldn't have even noticed if we were driving over a lake. I honestly wanted to go away and die.

CHAPTER SEVEN

Truth Be Told

When we got back to dad's house, I went straight to my bedroom and shut the door. I felt like I weighed a thousand pounds as I dropped onto the bed. By far, this was the worst day of my life.

I felt like I was the only person living on earth, no one seemed to be concerned about what I had gone through, nor did they care that I witnessed my dead baby mangled up on a silver metal tray, likely discarded as trash afterward. Had ANYONE asked me how the procedure went, they would have known I was dealing with tremendous grief. But no one did.

As I began to contemplate the significance of that morning, I started to experience intense cramping. My focus shifted to the pain in my gut, and I panicked as I felt blood trickle in my underwear. I didn't have a phone in my bedroom, so I tiptoed to the kitchen and called my friend, Cindy. Her mom is a nurse, and they lived a few houses away.

Cindy answered, and I asked her if her mom was home, she said yes. She was the only friend who knew I had an abortion that day and when I told her what was going on, she said I should walk over, and she'd inform her mom in the meantime.

As I slowly climbed the stairs to their house, her mom appeared in the doorway and ushered me in. We stood in the kitchen, and I almost barfed as the aroma of a mushroom dish hung in the air (I hated mushrooms then). She got right to the point and said Cindy told her what had happened earlier that day. She scolded me by saying, "If only you would have kept your legs closed or not had unprotected sex, you wouldn't be in this situation." Ouch, I did not expect that.

Her words were brutal and honest. Getting that off her chest, she went on to tell me the cramping is a normal side effect of abortion. She warned if I didn't lay low and rest, I could hemorrhage and end up in the ER, and I could even die.

This day could not get worse. I felt like I was sucker punched as I walked home with my head hung low. Maybe if I tried to run back, maybe I would hemorrhage, and maybe, just maybe I would die. Nah, I was in too much pain to consider all the drama of that idea.

I made it back without my dad and Paula even noticing that I was gone. I wondered if Cindy's mom was going to call them about my visit, but I never heard the phone ring.

Not only was this the worst day of my life, but it was also one of the most draining – mentally and physically. I took one of the muscle relaxers given to me earlier at the clinic and closed my eyes for a brief moment. Ten hours later, I woke up. You'd think that much sleep should've recharged me, but my heart hurt too much.

Though the cramping was all but gone, I stayed in bed most of the day and slept on and off. The remaining muscle relaxers not only helped me to sleep, but also to ward off the vivid image of my baby that I could not bear to think about anymore.

Come Monday morning; I would have to find a way to go to school and get distracted. As before, I placed my second abortion in the same compartment where I stored my first one; deep away in my mind with a lock and key. This plan worked before; I needed it to work again.

Outside of school, there wasn't much to do in the small town I felt trapped in. Drinking and smoking pot is how many high schoolers spent their free time. The friends I had made were of the partying type, and soon I was attending parties every weekend.

Drinking alcohol helped me to escape and keep my demons at bay. My sex addiction limited only with Shawn, so I needed to find another way to fill that void. The effects of alcohol helped me to forget that I was miserable and it tamped down the angsts I had over how messed up my life had become. After a few drinks, I transformed beautifully from "Debbie Downer" to "Lively Laura."

At one party, I met a cute guy named Jacob that I remembered seeing in my Science class. He struck up a conversation by asking me where I came from. I guess it was odd that I attended his high school for only the last few months of our senior year. Hmmm... if I told him the truth, I'd never see him again, and I'd be so embarrassed.

So I lied to Jacob and made up a story that I needed to stay with my dad to help with a private family matter. He bought it, and we started dating casually. Chivalry was alive in his manners as he held doors open for me when we went out. Jacob had a sweet smile and depth to his eyes. I felt safe with him, and often we'd lay on his lake pier at nighttime and watch the Northern lights for hours.

Shawn wasn't much on my mind at that time and for a good reason. I began to harbor bitterness toward him because he got to stay in our house when I was forced to live in a hick town three hours away. I didn't necessarily want him to suffer, but I thought it was unfair that I was the only one that was.

Meanwhile, my home life was dull and uneventful. I didn't talk much with Paula and my dad, there wasn't much to say. My life consisted of going to school, spending time with my new boyfriend, and drinking lots of alcohol.

Back in the 1980s, long distant phone calls were expensive. Most communication with family and friends back home was done with good old fashion pen and paper. The letters I received from my mom should have tore at my heart strings. Sadly, before being shipped up north, I had said awful things to her. I might have even said I hated her. She took the brunt of all the anger and confusion going on in my life.

One letter, in particular, helps me today to see how strained my relationships with my mother had become back then. Mom wrote, (verbatim)

My Lori, (during my rebellious teen years, I didn't want to be called Laura, so I unofficially changed my name to Lori and demanded everyone called me by this name)

I want you to know I love you, you are my daughter. I feel so left out of your life. I want what is best for you, and I pray you will be happy with dad. Talk things out with dad, he loves you too. Always remember Lori what you do with your life, keep your wits about yourself and remember your morals. You have time to grow up Lori, enjoy your life now. Date and have the right fun, someday you'll be happy for it. You're a pretty girl and could have a lot going for yourself. Slow down and take your time. You will grow up sooner than you think. Maybe in time you can tell me about Jeff. I want to tell you so much honey, but I've never been faced with a situation with you kids like this. I felt that I always had you kids and would never lose you. It's a very hard step for me honey, but if you can show me that you will be okay, I'll be okay. Write me Lori and let me know how things are going. I'll always be here for you. So many things are happening here. I only hope I can pull them all together. I love you all so much. Don't lose contact with your sisters and your brother Lori, they love you and will miss you. Also your relatives that love you too, especially grandma and grandpa. Keep your school habits

up, you did real good so far. Write your Aunt
Lynn, she really is a good aunt to you. She loves
you more than any other niece. She always felt
closer to you. Lori, you went through a rough
summer. Put it in the past and look for that star
that has your name on it and enjoy life. I felt
everything you went through this summer and
only wish that you and I could talk about it. I
want to understand you and help you honey. A
mother needs to be a part of the ups and downs of
her children. You've always been special to me
honey, I guess I always looked at you like I was
when I was your age. Please give me back my
Lori I had and want back so badly. If you are
happy Lori, I'll be happy. Don't close dad out.
Remember to say your prayers and go to church.
Pray to God to guide you. I'll pray too.
Remember always I love you and will miss you so
much and will always be here for you. - Mom

Sadly, I was so self-absorbed in my own misery
I could not understand my mom's pain. I couldn't
see that by shutting her and everyone else out of
my life; I was only pushing away people who loved

me and could and would help me. If only I would have let them in.

Instead of figuring out how to get back into the good graces of my family, I continued to party with my new friends. It was easier than facing the truth about Shawn. My family would never understand all we had done over the years. They still only suspected we might have fooled around a bit. No one knew the full truth, not yet.

Dealing with my family wasn't even a distant thought. Mentally, I had already checked out and was using alcohol to blot out every day before the one I was currently living. As long as I was home by curfew, dad didn't mind I was out with friends. Of course, he would have if he'd known how much I was drinking.

One night, I didn't make it home by curfew. In fact, I didn't come back at all until the morning. I spent the night at Jacob's house because his parents were out of town. He was the second boy to have sex with me. For many reasons, this experience was far different than with Shawn. The most significant was the use of a condom.

The entire night was not spent just having sex. We talked about funny things, serious things, and even scary things. In the middle of the night, Jacob made ice cream sundaes, and we ate them on his deck overlooking the lake, all the while wrapped up in a blanket together. In my young mind, I knew this was true romance and how girls are supposed to be treated.

As we watched the sunrise, I felt content and a bit happy. I couldn't remember the last time I felt happy about anything; other than when I knew I'd be able to drink and party. I wished I could have stayed there all weekend, but Jacob had to work. So we got dressed, and he drove me home. On the way, I rolled down the passenger side window and bent my head toward the refreshing breeze flowing through his truck. I was in a good mood for the first time in... I can't remember how long.

Well, until I walked through the front door and found my dad waiting for me with an angry and hot red face. Oh boy, I forgot to call him last night. This would result in being grounded, I concluded. He demanded to know where the hell

I was all night. I replied, "Why do you care?" Oops, that slipped out.

My words made him angrier. He responded, "Why do I care?" Which really wasn't a question for me, but the start of a rant about being a parent. "Because I'm your dad, because I love you, because I care about you, because I was worried you were hurt, or worse, dead." He went on and on. Jeez, I got it, I should have called.

Dad had a temper, but I do too, and as I stood in the foyer getting lambasted, my blood started to boil. He ruined my good mood, and I wanted to yell back. Instead, not meaning it, I grumbled an apology and promised it would never happen again. With that, he let me through, and I made a mental note to just pick up the damn phone to avoid this kind of conflict from happening again.

The next Friday, I screwed up again. I didn't call or come home by 11:00 pm. Instead, I whooped it up in the woods with my friends. I think I intended to be in bed by 11:01 pm; I didn't plan to break that rule, but the alcohol makes you forget.

On property tucked well away from the main roads, there stood a one-room hunting cabin with a fire pit and lawn chairs neatly lined up around the blaze. I estimated 40 teens were present and prepared for a good time. This was a larger crowd than the typical house parties I attended with Jacob. He was working, so I was on my own.

The dark stuff was calling my name; it was a brandy kind of night. I began by measuring two shots into my diet soda and topping it with three maraschino cherries speared on a sharp-edged sword. A short time later, it was too much work to go in the cabin to mix such a sissy strength drink. I surmised that all I needed was the brown bottle by itself.

Settling back by the fire, I placed the bottle between my legs to keep it safe (mostly from others). Like slugging from a bottle of beer, I drank the brandy in the same way. Had there been a brown bag surrounding its shape, I would have felt (and looked) like a hooligan.

The next thing I remember, though vaguely, was a man picking me up off the dirty ground and carrying me over his shoulder and into his truck. Was it Jacob? Did he get off work early?

Then suddenly I awoke the next morning in my bed. My head was pounding; I felt like I could die. Painfully, I tried to sit up as I searched my mind trying to remember how I got home. It couldn't have been Jacob; I would be in his bed, not mine.

Was it dad that found me? But how? How did he know where I was? Did one of my friends call him? Impossible, we were in the woods with no phone lines. Though it had to be him.

I felt nauseated as I stood up, each step forward was excruciating. But I had to find out what happened and why my memory was empty. I'd be grounded for sure; but how long depended on my dad filling in the blanks. I found him where he usually hung out, in his garage tinkering around.

To my surprise, he didn't seem upset with me. He asked how I was feeling. As if he couldn't tell by my body language, I said not very well. He looked amused as he told me I had a good 'ole hangover, and added that he wasn't surprised because I was totally wasted the night before. I was agitated that he found pleasure in my pain.

Dad explained when I missed curfew; he went looking for me. He drove around and stopped at a few gas stations in town and asked the storekeepers if they knew about any teenage parties going on. He said he was asking because he hadn't heard from his daughter since early in the morning and was worried about my whereabouts.

Finally, at his third stop, a young man said he knew about a big party located outside of the city limits in the woods. He gave my dad general directions and being that he was an avid hunter, he found the party. And then he found me face first in the dirt next to the fire with an empty bottle that once held cheap brandy clutched in my hand.

Dad calmly told me that because I had no sense of responsibility or desire to make right decisions, I was grounded indefinitely. He said not only could no one else at the party see the dangerous situation I was in, no one could have helped because they were all as shit-faced as me. To drive his point home, he said no one even noticed when he took me away. Instead of waking up in my bed that morning, I could have been kidnapped and maybe even be dead.

Putting it that way, I guess things could have gone south quickly. As I turned to get to a toilet to spill my guts, he said one more thing. The next time I broke a rule, he was sending me to a group home or detention facility, whichever place would take me first. Now that was an address I did not want to have and judging by his tone, a threat I took to heart.

I spent the rest of the day either in bed or next to the toilet bowl. It was the worst hangover I'd ever experienced. The short spell of escape that alcohol gave me hardly seemed worth all the physical suffering I was going through that day. What was I doing to myself? My drinking habit was out of control. Drinking a fifth of cheap brandy wasn't solving my problems, alcohol was making things worse.

The rest of my senior year, I became a hermit. Whether dad meant what he said or not, I didn't want to drink much anymore. Jacob and I fizzled out; it's hard to have a relationship when you are grounded. We remained friends, and sometimes we chatted by our lockers about Science projects or other small talks.

Oddly, I wasn't heartbroken with our break-up because my heart still belonged to Shawn. As hard as I tried to forget about him, we had a past, and we never finished writing our story. Forces beyond our control abruptly stopped it. Did we have another chapter to begin, together, forever? Would our family circumstances write our ending for us? I wished I had a fortune teller to show me the future.

Every day I did my best to stay out of trouble. I had all but secluded myself from the outside world and only ventured out when I had to go to school or go to my new part-time job at Dairy Queen. Occasionally, I'd walk over to visit Cindy or she would come to visit me. Still, I had no interest in being a part of anything else. I'm certain now that I was clinically depressed at the time.

One boring night, as I sat in my room listening to the radio, 80s love ballets played over and over, each one of them reminding me of Shawn and how much I missed him. My heart ached to be with him; I felt so alone with our secrets. Some unknown force compelled me to pick up a pen and paper and write our story down. I was tired of it being locked up in my mind, and I needed to get it out.

My words filled up only a page and a half. The format was more of a timeline with a few caveats sprinkled in for emphasis as necessary:

- Lost my virginity at fourteen with Shawn.
- Fooled around countless times with no protection against pregnancy until I turned sixteen.
- Didn't get my period, faked being raped to cover up our relationship.
- Received the official word that I was pregnant on my sixteenth birthday.
- Had my first abortion days later.
- Continued having sex with Shawn, still didn't use protection.
- Mom almost caught us, we were separated, but we still found a way to have sex.
- Got pregnant again, blamed Jeff, who didn't exist.
- Had my second abortion at the beginning of my second trimester – I was seventeen.

Wow, that turned out to be a bit therapeutic as I wrote the last bullet point down. However, as long as that paper remained in my possession, I was still alone with our skeletons. What if I mailed it to a friend back home? Nah, they wouldn't understand. What if I mailed it to one of my sisters? No, they would tell mom. Aunt Lynn would tell my mom too. Then I thought of mom's friend Tammy who drove me to get my first abortion. She was perfect, she'd be unbiased and would keep my secret safe.

I took a fresh page and wrote a quick preface, explaining what the next two pages were about (as if she could not deduce this on her own). I wrote that I had secrets which were eating me alive and I needed someone else to know them. I also wrote that I loved Shawn and hoped to be with him again, someday. I folded the three pages together, addressed an envelope, placed a stamp in upper right corner and put it next to my book bag to mail in the morning.

When I dropped it in the mailbox on my way to school, I felt a release as I opened the metal door and shoved it in. It didn't cross my mind that anyone other than Tammy would read it.

A few days later, the phone rang, and after a while, dad yelled for me to pick up the line in the living room. His voice seemed higher pitched than normal as he said mom needed to talk to me. His tone made me nervous, and anxiety raced through my veins as I walked toward the phone. Each step, I was trying to plot how to get out of the letter, wondering what lies I could tell. She must have read the letter, why else would Dad sound so serious?

After I had said hello, I heard dad drop off the call, and without skipping a beat, mom told me she read my letter to Tammy. My instinct for lying my way out of it was gone. I didn't want to lie. I couldn't lie, I was done with lying.

Tammy shared the letter with my mom out of concern for me, so she said. There was nothing else for me to say, except that I was sorry. I was sorry for all the lies and deceit, I was sorry for all problems and pain, I was sorry for letting grandpa and grandma down, for letting Aunt Lynn down and my siblings. But I was most sorry for letting her down.

There was a pause on the phone line; I almost thought we lost our connection until she replied, "What's done is done Lori, it's time to move on." She didn't scream at me, didn't judge me, and didn't condemn me. What she merely implied was, this is a new day, a new beginning.

With that, we exchanged 'I love you' and ended the call. I went back to my room and stood at the window. I stared at nothing for a long time. My mind was calm, and I felt as if a hundred millstones had been lifted from around my neck. Could it have been that easy all along? Was the truth the only way to set a soul free? Was I off the hook, for everything?

At that moment, I didn't need those answers; I had no more secrets to weigh me down. I prayed Shawn would understand that I wasn't selling him out; I couldn't carry the burdens of our sins all by myself anymore. I knew it was more than I could handle and I needed my family back.

My senior year ended on a high note when I learned I'd be able to get my high school diploma from my hometown and graduate with my original class. It seemed like things were looking up for me, finally.

CHAPTER EIGHT

Time to be a Big Girl

Graduation came with no fanfare. I may have had enough credits to graduate, but I had no clue where my life was heading. I spent my high school years squandering away opportunities to get smarter and figure out who I wanted to be when I grew up.

Marquette University in Milwaukee was the only college name I knew, and this was because I spent a weekend with a "Big Sister" (from Big Brothers, Big Sisters of America) as part of a mentoring program when I was in sixth grade. College was as foreign to me as was a "normal" teenage life.

As my friends were stocking up on dorm treasures like mini refrigerators, toaster ovens, coffee makers, and monogrammed laundry bags, I was staring straight at a blank future.

To makes matters worse, I wasn't turning eighteen until September. Not being a full-fledged adult meant I couldn't move out on my own yet. Going home was out of the question because Shawn still had two years of high school. Bunking with my dad was my numero uno option.

One ray of light came at the end of that summer. With all the antics I was entangled in over the past years, I never got around to getting a driver's license. As I inched my way closer to my eighteenth birthday, dad started teaching me how to drive.

For practice, we used Paula's brown Nissan Datsun, a manual transmission. Dad tried to keep his cool as I ground the gears like the amateur I was in the first few weeks of driving in the city. However, practice makes perfect, and soon my shifting was a synchronized masterpiece.

On my eighteenth birthday, I took the road test and passed with flying colors. As vain as I was, I didn't even care that the picture made me look stoned on my new license. I grabbed it from the lady behind the counter and ran outside to show my dad. He was patiently waiting, leaning up against the Datsun. As I approached the little brown car, I realized that I could not have done it without him.

A strange feeling was stirring around inside of me; an appreciation and gratefulness for my dad. I thought, "Was this a sign of maturity?"He let me drive home, and as I sped up to the 55 MPH posted limit on Highway A, I felt sorry for all the crap I'd put him through. I even felt sorry for giving Paula so much grief.

Just like mom, I never gave them a fair chance. Deep down I blamed them for all the misery in my life; I didn't know where else to point the finger. I wasn't ready to look in the mirror and see the truth, not yet.

With license in hand, I was able to find a job without working around Paula and my dad's schedules. After a few weeks, dad helped me buy my first car - a 1975 Buick Electra 4-door which was as big as a house boat. I didn't care how giant it was; it got me a new job at a nice supper club. I waitressed and earned great tips.

Although I didn't know quite what constituted being a full-fledged adult, I felt like I was becoming one. I had a new goal - save enough money to move back home. The ultimate prize would be to live closer to Shawn. Lord help me, but my heart still belonged to him. I desperately wanted to know if we had a future. I had some doubts, though.

One of my sisters told me that he had been dating other girls. As sad as this made me feel, I couldn't blame him. I sold him out and left him to swim with the sharks; threw him under the bus and left him for dead. He lived in hell after my confession and got labeled a perpetrator. I wasn't even sure he ever wanted to see my face again. However, I wanted to see his.

It turns out I'd get my answer soon enough, as my dad and Paula were moving to the Sunshine

State. They had been wanting to make a move south for years and finally got a chance to follow that dream.

Even though I had saved some money, I did not have near enough to venture out on my own. My older sister Kelly and I talked about getting an apartment together, but she wasn't ready either. Moving home was out, so I turned to the very people on whom I'd inflicted that whopper of a lie summers before.

Aunt Lynn and Uncle Ryan are best described as big-hearted. They'd give the shirts off their backs for you if you needed one. They also were merciful with me after I wrecked that summer for them and my cousins. It didn't surprise me when I was allowed to move in with them until I got a place of my own. A clean slate was offered up, and I took it.

On one condition... that I'd have to pay room and board. I accepted and soon found a waitressing job at a nearby family restaurant. After a couple of weeks, I was able to start paying them.

Then my scheming began again. I had to find a way to meet up with Shawn. Now that the family knew about us, it would be near impossible to be alone. But, where there is a will, there is always a way. And I had an unyielding will.

Living only a few miles away from each other helped, and having my own car was icing on the cake. No more Greyhound Buses for this girl. Even though patience is not one of my strong suits, I knew I had to wait for the right time. Jumping the gun and getting caught would do us no good. So I enlisted the help of Kelly because she still lived at home and had access to Shawn.

Since moving back, I sometimes went "clubbing" in Milwaukee with Kelly and her boyfriend. Even though I was not legally allowed to drink alcohol, I got in with a borrowed ID. One of Kelly's friends had dark hair as I did, and although this was the only thing similar, it worked every time.

The saying, "Good things come to those who wait" was so true when Kelly told me Shawn leaped at the chance to go clubbing with us. As a bonus, he was sleeping over at his best friend's house, and I was invited to join him.

My hands were shaky as I put mascara on and curled my hair. I was all grown up since the last time Shawn and I were alone, and I wanted to be as pretty as possible for him. As I pulled up my tightest pair of jeans, I felt as though I was getting ready for a real date. Our first public appearance as lovers, ever.

The clean slate mentality applied to us as well. That night as I hopped into the backseat of Kelly's car, the shame and guilt from the past few years disappeared when I plopped down next to Shawn.

He had to have heard my heart beating fast as I turned my body into his for a hug. We smiled at each other, and with knowing eyes, like every time before, we knew we'd be intimate in no time.

Thankfully, the club was packed. Being busy made it easier to get in with a fake ID because the bouncers got easily distracted by all the commotion. Shawn did not have an ID, so I planned to use the wet ink from my hand stamp and press it upon his skin. I'd seen it work for others, but I had to be quick.

The club sat within a bowling alley and to enter it, we had to walk through a spacious foyer.

This is where Shawn nervously paced and waited for my return. With fake ID in hand, I gave my best smile to the bouncer as he took Kelly's friend's license and glanced at the birthdate. Apparently, the date was all he cared about as he stamped my hand and nodded me through.

Quickly I did an about-face, rambling that I forgot my money in the car and high-tailed it to press my stamp onto Shawn's left hand. Like magic, it worked. He waited for a crowd of people to blend in with, and as he came upon the bouncer, he casually scanned his hand under the special light and was waved in. It worked!

We had an epic time and danced most of the night; taking only a few beverage breaks to catch our breath. The music was so loud my skin jumped, and the strobe lights made our dance moves seem like we were drunker than we were. We were disappointed when the warning lights flashed telling us it would soon be closing time.

Aunt Lynn thought I was staying at a friend's house as I climbed into bed with Shawn in a spare bedroom at his buddy's house. His parents were away for the weekend, so we had free reins to have all the fun we wanted without getting caught. We experienced another first, sleeping together in the same bed for an entire night.

In the morning, I woke first and propped my elbow on the pillow to watch Shawn sleep. As I gazed at him, I wondered if he loved me as much as I loved him. We never talked about the "L-word"; we weren't that sophisticated yet. After a few minutes, I woke him up so that we could fool around before I had to leave for work. I was on cloud nine the entire drive back, and I felt happiness bursting at my seams.

After that rendezvous, we tried to get together as often as we could get away with being alone. We had a perfect opportunity one afternoon when our parents left for the Milwaukee Brewer's "opening day" game. They never missed it and would be gone for hours. For whatever reasons, our siblings weren't home either.

It was April 7, 1986, I opened the front door to our family house and entered the living room to find Shawn standing by the couch, munching on an apple. He said hello and asked how much time I had. I replied that I had to be back by 4:00

pm because my shift started at 5:00 pm. It was about 1:00 pm.

Remarkably, we were still using the "pull-out" technique, and it seemed to be working because my periods kept coming on time. Though our luck was about to run out yet again. I'll never understand why we were so casual about our sex; never giving pregnancy a first or second thought. Especially after the abortions.

Afterward, I had a weird premonition and told Shawn that this hook-up made me pregnant again. He shrugged off my concern and said I was paranoid because of our past. Silently I said, "No, you are wrong," and then out loud I said, "Goodbye." As I stammered out of the door, he asked me to call him after work, and I gave him a thumbs up in agreement and hopped in my car.

On the drive back, I prayed I was wrong about getting pregnant. Then I thought about how much I hated that our relationship was a secret again and I couldn't stand the spontaneity of our intimacy anymore. I wanted what we had at the club; freedom to be together and express our desire and love for one another.

I never called him after work that night. Several weeks went by as I picked up extra shifts at the restaurant. The more I worked, the faster I could get my place, or one with Kelly. By this time, my period was late, and it was never late. Remember? It was never late, unless...

Getting Shawn on the phone was only possible if no one was at home when I called. I got lucky one afternoon and told him my period hadn't come yet. He replied I needed to give it a couple of weeks more before we panicked. So, I waited. It still didn't come. So I bought a pregnancy test for the second time in my life.

It was déjà vu. This had happened before, right? It was the same scenario as before. I locked myself in the bathroom at my aunt and uncle's house and patiently waited to see if the stick turned blue. It did. I was pregnant again, for the third time in 18 short years of life. How had I, how had we, let this happen *again*?

Oddly, I didn't panic as I had done previously. I called one of my friends, Jenny, and asked if she could pick me up to hang out. She didn't hesitate, and within the hour, she honked, and I jumped in her car. She asked, "Where to?" and I replied, "wherever you want to go."

We exchanged some small talk, and as we briefly sat at a stop sign, I blurted out that I was pregnant. Jenny looked over at me to see that I was serious. She pulled the car over to the side of the next street, and asked, "Is it Shawn's?" I replied flatly, "Yes." By then, most of my friends knew about Shawn and me.

Jenny calmly said, "Well obviously, you can't keep it, it will ruin your life." Wearing her friend counselor hat, she went on to say my life was just beginning and that I had no choice but to get an abortion.

She didn't know about my other two abortions, none of my friends back home did. Only my close friend Cindy from up north knew. I was too ashamed and embarrassed to tell anyone else about them. Jenny had no clue that I had already gone down that hell hole before.

In defiance, I told her I was keeping my baby. I felt the need to resist what she was offering as my solution; the "easy" way out yet again. She replied, "I think you are making a mistake, but I support you no matter what." I wasn't in the mood to drive around anymore, so I asked her to take me back to my aunt and uncle's house.

As I sat on my bed, the words from the so-called therapy session with Jenny were swirling around in a last ditch effort to take root. What did she know about tough choices? She had a normal life. Her original parents were still married. Her three brothers were her blood relation. She used birth control when she had sex. Jenny would never need to consider abortion because she would never let herself get pregnant.

What I would have done to be Jenny at that moment. Looking around at my surroundings snapped me back to reality. I wasn't normal as she was. I was banned from my family house because of an insatiable love affair with my stepbrother. I've been pregnant each year for the last three years of my young life. In just four years, I've lived in three different zip codes and went to three high schools. All because I couldn't keep my legs closed.

The subdued values from my Catholic upbringing were coming alive and giving me a reason to take a stand. Yes, now I remember – Thou Shall Not Kill. There wasn't a snowball's chance in hell I'd enter a grim reaper abortion clinic again. I couldn't do it and I wouldn't. My decision was final; I was going to have this baby.

Now I had to share the news. I found Aunt Lynn at the breakfast bar reading the local newspaper and drinking a glass of milk. This was a ritual; her "me" time, I surmised. At pregnancy number three, you'd think it would be easy for me to tell my aunt I was pregnant again. Like a little girl confessing I broke a pretty china plate, I nervously told her my news.

Although I do not recall the exact words she spoke, she did throw her support behind the decision to keep my baby. Whew, that wasn't so bad, I thought. One down, two more to go. Mom and Shawn were next.

My mom took the news better than I feared. Though I cannot remember her exact words either, abortion was not one of them this time around. She accepted my choice and told me that things would work out in the long run. I believed this too.

Last, but not least, I told Shawn. I knew my news would not reel in any support from him, but he deserved to know. His reaction was casual and non-committed. He said he didn't know what to think or say. He mumbled something about being powerless and much too young to be a dad. Besides, we both believed our family would stand in our way of being together.

Sadly, at that point, there was nothing else we could say to each other. Shawn may not have had any power, but I did. I was an adult now, and I'd make it on my own. I was making a different choice this time. I owned this so-called decision.

It was time to be a big girl and soon, a mom.

CHAPTER NINE

Miss

Independent

If I was going to pull off a "big girl" act, I had some "big people" things to figure out. Like where to live and how to pay for adult things like rent, utilities, phone, and food. My waitressing pay could maybe stretch enough to cover a phone bill. But $2.00 an hour at a

"Denny's" style restaurant would hardly put food on my table or pay rent.

I'd like to say I choose to move back to Milwaukee for nostalgia. After all, this is where my mom began her single parent journey. Rather, I chose Milwaukee because of the transit system. You see, dad told me I "ain't gonna have my car for very long if I didn't take care of it." Following advice from any adult, not only my dad was a rarity for me in those days. As luck would have it, my "big boat on wheels" died on the side of a road after work one night. Off to the boneyard, it went.

Coincidently, my new place sat directly across the street from grandma and grandpa's old house. This had to be a good omen. I reasoned if my mom could do it in that neighborhood, I could do it too.

My apartment, or should I say, my *unit* for the sheer tiny size of it, was tucked away up on the third floor of a huge and ancient house. The stairs leading up to it were wooden and worn, and the walls in the hallway still bore the original but faded green paint. I had neighbors up on floor three with me. A young couple I only knew existed on early weekend mornings around 2:00 am by way of loud bumping music, and the wafts of pot smoke seeping through the cracks of my front and only door.

The best thing about my unit was the antique claw foot bathtub. I had only seen them on TV and thought it was stylish. The rest of my living space consisted of a kitchen/living room, a small bedroom, and tiny bathroom where the claw foot bathtub took up most of the space. The whole place was dreary and made up of pale off-white painted walls. The carpet was worn and thin and had likely not seen a cleaner for many moons.

There were also little rodents living with me up on my floor. I didn't see much of them, only when I left food out. Boy, they loved apple pie. One morning I found a few feasting on a pie Aunt Lynn had made for me. It must have been the most delicious pie because it took a broom on their rumps to scatter them away.

How was I able to pay for this lap of luxury? Welfare. I had also signed up for food stamps and Medicaid. At the start, Aunt Lynn had a hand in helping me too. She had kept my room and board money and gave it back to me for the security deposit and first month's rent. Yeah, she is amazing like that.

Welfare sucked. I hated being poor. I wanted my baby to sleep in a crib with a beautiful flowing canopy fencing her in, ever so gently. I envisioned lovely sheets, pillows, and blankets surrounding her in comfort as she peacefully slept.

Instead, she got a used crib from one of my cousins with plastic-like bumpers to prevent her feet and arms from falling through the sides. Even the hanging animal mobile was a hand-me-down.

The neighborhood was roughly the same as it had been in my youth. McDonald's was still on Twenty-Fifth Street. The resale shop where we bought Christmas gifts for my mom, Purple Heart, was still on National Avenue. And my most favorite place was in the same spot too, Central Library.

Being in that library made me feel like I was inside a castle. Built in 1898, it showcased lavish mosaic tiles and marble floors, vaulted ceilings, pillars, and brass and stained glass light fixtures. I felt like a princess when I entered those giant oak and mahogany doors. Each floor housed books waiting to be lifted off their assigned spot and placed into my hands for consumption.

The best part of going to the library was it was free. I spent most of my time pouring over pages on how to be a superior parent. More to the point, a best *single* parent. Books on healthy pregnancy were a good read for me too, seeing I was expanding rapidly.

The church was also mostly free and another place I enjoyed immensely. Like so many things in my old neighborhood, the same Catholic Church and school I attended in my youth were in the same location.

As I walked under the archway and through the vestibule for the first time since my eighth grade graduation ceremony, I felt peace surround me. I quietly sat in the first available pew where I didn't have to crawl over anyone to sit. "God, it feels awesome to be in Your home again," I silently told Him.

It had been too long. So much time that I couldn't even use a month as a reference, it was years. Thankfully, attending Catholic Mass is like riding a bike. You don't forget all the moving parts it takes to get through it, no matter how long it has been.

Once the opening song began, I blended right in and sang without even having to look at the hymnal. During the sermon, my mind drifted (as it does so many times during this part of Mass) to the classrooms next door where I spent six years of my youth, mostly as a normal kid.

My heart ached for simplicity like that again. Heck, I wouldn't even mind Sr. John Fischer back in my life if I could be a kid again. Now my life was anything but simple. The last box I packed into the U-Haul a mere five years ago changed what simple would be forever more.

The move westward transformed me from mostly normal to out of control. Now I was a pregnant 18-year old who was lonely, afraid, and uncertain about the journey I was on. As the months marched on, I went through a short period of cold feet and tried to convince myself that my baby needed two parents, not a single mom on welfare.

I began to consider adoption. I rationalized that my baby deserved a nursery not only with a canopy but also with the matching curtains.

Didn't she? What on earth could I give her? At present, only an itty-bitty so called apartment with pot smoking neighbors and mice that feasted on my desserts.

The idea of adoption came to a screeching halt one Sunday morning at Mass. As I walked through the archway, I spotted a baby in the vestibule clothed in bright white. Seeing this, I almost turned around and left, as this meant a Baptism would be getting worked into Mass. We Catholics know Baptisms always add at least 20 minutes more to the service.

However, that would have been rude since the mother made eye contact with me and smiled as she moved her eyes to my protruding belly. So I smiled back and took a seat.

As Father poured Holy Water over the baby's head, and as the baby cried out a lung, my hands dropped to my belly. My own baby had my full attention as she pushed and pulled around. She hadn't been that active, ever. Was it what I had for breakfast? Was it the baby's cries she heard? The cries were so loud; I'm sure people driving outside could hear them, even with the windows rolled up!

As I listened to the commitment the parents and godparents were publically accepting, I concluded why my baby was doing summersaults. She was sending me a message that only I could hold her over the baptismal font on her Christening day. She didn't want a wealthy married couple; she wanted me.

My baby's gymnastics kicked me back to reality. What on earth was I thinking? I survived my tumultuous teenage years, to what, throw in the towel? A flashback of my uncle's sentiments came to mind, "Someday you will help make this world a better place." Was this what he meant? I had to admit that the creation of life is pretty spectacular. And my own hands could help form such a masterpiece; a human life. Me, I had this opportunity. Figuratively speaking, I could be an artist. From that moment on, I put to bed the idea of adoption and never thought about it again.

As I neared the six-month mark, my doctor ordered an ultrasound. After drinking more water than I thought my body could hold (for the test to work), I laid back on the table as the technician swayed a magic wand up and down and side to side across my bulging belly.

My eyes were delighted to meet my work of art; my masterpiece on the imaging screen. I said something about technology coming a long way as the technician pointed to my baby's thigh area and asked if I wanted to know the sex. I said, yes. And she said from what she could see (or couldn't see, no penis) – I was having a girl.

Things got real that day. A tiny human was not only growing inside me; she was one hundred percent dependent on me. She was living and breathing because of my choice to keep her, and I saw the significance of this through a magic wand.

What I would have done to share this experience with Shawn. For that matter, with anyone. Even though the ultrasound proved I was not alone on this journey, I felt a ping of loneliness. I longed to share the printed images I received from the technician as I sat up to get dressed. But it was just she and me; no one else was at my side.

To my surprise, my family threw a baby shower when I was eight months pregnant. I was excited that not all my baby's things would be second-hand. We played the traditional baby bingo, how big is mommy's tummy and baby trivia. I felt blessed because many family members came to support my decision. Shawn was nowhere to be seen, though, and this made me sad.

Not even a month later, I went into labor at around 6:00 pm on January 12, 1987. I called my labor coach, a good friend of my family, and she raced over, and we sped to the hospital. The doctor examined me and said I was only 4 cm dilated and it would be awhile until things got serious. This news was disappointing, so I asked, "How long do you think?" He responded, "Hard to say, it's your first, so it'll likely be hours."

I'd have my baby at a Catholic hospital, St. Francis. The walls were plain, and the lights were dim. In those days, there weren't any fancy labor and delivery rooms like today. You gave birth in the delivery room under a metal chandelier, and I recall my legs were strapped down so that I couldn't tumble off onto the shiny white floor during labor. The surroundings were blasé to say the most.

The nurse encouraged me to sleep; she said I needed my strength for labor. Yeah right, I thought. I've been waiting nine long months for this day; I wasn't closing my eyes for anything. But I told her I would give it a try, just to be respectful.

After a few hours, my friend and I walked up and down the drab corridors trying to help labor along. Every so often, I'd have to stop and grab hold of whatever solid fixture was within reach, and "Lamaze" through the wretched pain called a contraction.

Finally, my water broke, and I was officially in labor. A nurse helped me get up on a gurney and then I was whisked away to the delivery room. The pain was so intense; I thought I was going to die. The Lamaze breathing wasn't helping so I stopped trying altogether.

Kayla was born at 10:31 a.m. The doctor yelled out, "It's a sweet, beautiful girl" as he lifted her up for me to get a quick peak. I thought, what a head of hair she has! He handed her off to a nurse on standby for a quick clean and exam. The sound of her wailing was music to my ears.

It's almost cliché to say, but the pain from labor was all but gone. Unfortunately, Kayla developed a fever during labor so I could not hold her right away. The nurse assured me it was precautionary, just long enough to bring her temperature down. Not being able to cradle her was wicked in my mind, and I scoffed at this decision and demanded to hold her.

The doctor came over and asked, "You don't want her to get sicker, do you?" I said, "Of course not," and he replied, "then she needs to be isolated until her fever is under control." I conceded and cried. The nurse took me back to my room, and I laid in bed praying she was going to be alright.

It didn't take long until I fell asleep; I had been up for 30 hours straight, and I simply crashed. A few hours later familiar voices woke me; my family had arrived. Wearily I scanned the room to see who came to visit and got emotional when my eyes came across my mom. I desperately needed her approval and reassurance that everything was going to work out.

She came over to the side of my bed, hugged me, and said she was proud of me. Happy tears came, I needed to hear those words at that exact moment from my mom. She went on to say that her granddaughter was beautiful. Wait, she saw her already? Yes, she said, but only through the window of the nursery.

At that moment, the nurse came to check on me, and I asked her if my baby's fever had gone down. She said yes and asked if I wanted to go to the nursery to officially meet my baby. Ecstatic, I said, "Let's go!" and she helped me out of bed.

We didn't find Kayla in her baby bin with our name pinned to the outside. Instead, a nurse was rocking her in a cozy area in the nursery and humming a song while gently stroking her head. The nurse was a large white woman with Mrs. Beasley glasses perched on the end of her nose. She had kind eyes that looked up and said, "You must be mom, would like to hold your daughter?"

The smile on my face was her answer, and she stood and placed her in my arms.

Kayla was beautiful, just like mom said. She had olive skin coloring, a full head of dark hair and long dainty fingers that reminded me of a pianist. I couldn't see much of the rest of her body because the nurse wrapped her tightly in a blanket, like a little cocoon. But she was perfect in size, 6lbs, and 11oz.

As she opened her eyes, my heart melted as I saw a pool of blue with hints of brown. She was a masterpiece and a most precious gift from God. As I rocked Kayla and hummed the "Hush Little Baby" lullaby, I knew my life was forever changed.

Another nurse helped me bring her back to my room so that my family could meet her. They took turns holding her, and after a while, they left so that I could get some rest. Before leaving, I asked my mom if Shawn knew that our daughter was born and she said she thought so. Sadly, there would be no visits from him during our hospital stay, nor afterward when we went home.

It had been such a lonely time in my life, and now I could see it was not for nothing. I had a new purpose, and I wouldn't have much time to be lonesome anymore. Even though I still dreamed of a day when Shawn and I (and now Kayla) would be together, I was a mom now and needed to get on with this new life.

My grandparents brought us home from the hospital. When we got there, some of my family greeted us at the door. It was a pleasant surprise and helped ease the slight anxiety which was creeping into my mood. I hoped I was ready to do this. I needed to do this. She needed me to do this. Could I do this?

We visited for a while, and after a bit, they left so that we could settle in. I was sad to see them leave and wished they didn't live so far away.

CHAPTER TEN

Second Chances

O n March 22, 1987, Kayla received the Holy Sacrament of Baptism. This would be the formal commitment to keep God at the center of her upbringing. I asked Aunt Lynn, who'd always been there for me to be her Godmother and I asked my brother, David, to be her Godfather. David, a quiet yet honorable man, can always be counted on to do what is right and is forever loyal to family. Between the both of them, I knew if something ever happened to me, they would take care of Kayla and raise her well.

My grandmother made Kayla's christening dress from my mom's first wedding dress, and it was gorgeous. Kayla's olive skin against the vintage lace made the dress more stunning. Most of my family was present on this special day. Although Shawn's name appeared on the Baptism Certificate, he did not attend.

It didn't take long to feel how draining being a single parent can be. I quickly learned when my baby slept, I slept. There was no room for selfishness, and I needed to be on my game every day. Although my days were busy and filled with diaper changing, formula making, rocking, bathing, and other mom activities, slowly Shawn crept back into my mind. I wanted him to be a part of all the newness going on in my life.

After a few months, Kelly and I were finally following through on our plans to get an apartment together. She had a good job and was willing to split the cost of living with me. By the end of April that year, we found a two-bedroom apartment about three miles from our family home. David and Uncle Ryan helped move us out of Milwaukee and into a new opportunity to be closer to Shawn.

Kelly enjoyed spending time with Kayla, which was helpful because it gave me small breaks to search for a job. Welfare was not going to cut it for me anymore; it was too difficult to survive on. It wasn't going to get me a vehicle I needed now that I didn't have a transit system to utilize.

Shortly after the move west again, I learned that Shawn had been dating a girl for some time. He was finishing high school, and soon he would be 18 years old. Unbeknownst to me, he was knee deep in his relationship with this girl, and she was pregnant.

Even though she had a miscarriage, I was shocked to learn they were going to get married anyway. The day after Shawn turned 18, they wedded. To say I was outraged is an understatement. How could he marry someone else? I had given him his first child! I had been pregnant with his child not just once, but three damn times! I couldn't comprehend what was happening. I didn't see how I would be able to be with him now.

After this devastating news, I tried to keep my wits about me. After all, I had a daughter, and she needed me sane. I was finally able to get a full-time job at a local accounting firm as a secretary. A woman in our apartment building also had a daughter about the same age as mine and began babysitting for me.

Every day I did my best to move on from my past with Shawn. Had we not shared a child together, perhaps this may have been easier. Even though I was starting to come around to the understanding that he and I didn't seem destined to be, my heart still belonged to him, and I couldn't figure out how to release that hold.

Shortly after his wedding, Shawn contacted me and announced that he wanted to see Kayla. At first, I had mixed feelings. I didn't care to see him with a ring on his finger, or see him with another woman. But then I thought about Kayla and knew she deserved to know her daddy. I said, sure and we set a date and time.

For the first visit, Shawn came into my apartment and spent time with Kayla while his wife waited in their car. I was not about to let him take her without first getting comfortable with him. He played with her for a while until I thought she would be fine to go with him.

Though she wasn't thrilled to leave the apartment without me, she did go without too much drama. After the door shut, I quickly went to the window and peered out as he placed her in the backseat, safely in a car seat. I should have been happy Shawn wanted to be a part of Kayla's life. Instead, I was sulky that he wasn't intimately part of mine anymore.

For each subsequent time Shawn picked up Kayla for visits, the sexual tension between us was growing. One visit he came alone, and we did the unthinkable. We put Kayla down for a nap, and we had sex. Had we lost our minds? What if Kayla woke and found us in such a particular way? What if his wife found out?

That visit was all it took for the dam to break and for us to fall back into old habits. Shawn started visiting more often, and each time we made sure it was during Kayla's naptime. It didn't take long before I began to question why we were taking crazy chances again. Life changed, we both had responsibilities we didn't have before. My primary focus was Kayla, and he should have had his desires only with his wife.

It mattered to me that he was married and I was getting tired of him going back home to her after each rendezvous with me. I did not want to be his secret lover anymore, that arrangement always ended with regret and a broken heart. I had to make him understand. Otherwise, it was over. The next time we were together, I gave him an ultimatum.

A few days later, I told him I didn't want to continue having sex with him anymore. I said it wasn't right and I didn't want to share him with his wife. I warned him that I would tell her if we didn't stop. As I said those words, I knew they were pointless, and we unclothed and jumped on the couch.

Neither one of us could stop. We knew what we were doing was wrong, but we'd been doing this for far too long, and old habits are the hardest to break. I half-heartedly kept on harping at him, and eventually, he was forced to make a decision.

It turned out his wife was pregnant again, and he decided to come clean with her. I was confident she would kick him to the curb, and he would declare his love for me finally. Besides, was she planning on never letting him see Kayla again? The chances are we would get together at some point in the future if she forgave him. Then what?

To my surprise, Shawn called me and informed me he and his wife were going to work things out. He said they needed time to figure out how visitation would go down in the future. For now, he would not be able to spend time with Kayla if I was around.

In other words, once again, I was getting pushed out of his life. This time, not from our parents, but from his wife. In all fairness to her, she had no idea who she was dealing with. I was not simply going to go away. How long had she dated Shawn, a year? We were intimate for seven years and been through storms she couldn't comprehend. No, I wasn't going away, this was a promise.

Instead, I took a pen and paper and wrote about our love affair. All the sordid details spilled over on the college-ruled notebook paper I still had from high school. My love for Shawn would not be threatened, not by anyone. The letter was anonymous, written in the third person so no one would know I could be so vindictive.

When I finished, I folded the pages, put them in an envelope and mailed my anonymous version of a confession to his wife's parent's house. My last chance with him was on the line, and I hoped I could count on her parents to put an end to what I felt was a sham marriage.

After I had dropped the letter in a mailbox, I felt a tinge of regret and second-guessed what I had done. I did not want to hurt Shawn; I only wanted us to have a fair chance in a real relationship. We never were able to give it a legitimate try, and I didn't want to go through the rest of my life wondering if we were meant to be together.

Though I didn't hear it directly from Shawn, I did find out her parents stepped in and demanded a separation. She moved back home, and Shawn stayed in their apartment. His failed marriage should have been a celebratory time for me, but I actually felt sorry for Shawn. I didn't want to cause him pain, and it turns out his life would get ugly for a while.

We talked on the phone shortly after their separation, and he asked why I wrote the letter. I denied I did, but he said he knew it was me. We got into an intense argument, and I can't remember who hung up the phone first, but it ended abruptly.

Soon after this, he lost his job, his apartment, and he was not allowed to move back home with our parents. He was even homeless for a spell. Kelly would never allow him to move in with us, so his grandpa took him in.

Not surprisingly, tension in our family was high. I had an underlying agitation over what was happening, or not happening between Shawn and me. One night, I got a call from my old friend, Marie, asking if I wanted to come to Milwaukee to celebrate her 21st birthday. It seemed like a great way to get all the craziness off my mind, so I said yes.

It was the dead of winter and freezing cold, even for Wisconsin. I talked Kelly into babysitting, and I headed to Milwaukee to party. We celebrated Marie's birthday at her favorite tavern, packed with handsome young men. The music was so loud we could hardly hold a conversation.

It didn't matter though because we spent most of the night on the dance floor. The drinks were steady and strong. Time flew by too fast, and we moaned in disappointment when the lights flickered, warning that closing time was upon us.

We were both drunk as we hugged goodbye. As I stumbled to find the car, I yelled to Marie to drive safely and call in the morning.

I vaguely remember finding the car, getting behind the wheel, and starting it up to get warm. It was well after 2:00 am, and it was as cold as I ever remembered it could be. Somehow I made it to the interstate but took a wrong exit, about 15 miles short of the right one. I dimly remember stopping for directions, but the gas station was not open.

The next thing I remember, I was approaching a "T" on the road and needed to turn right or left. Instead, I kept going straight. The car launched about 60 feet and rolled three times, and I was ejected during the second turn. Had I not been, I would not be writing these words.

As I lay on the frozen field, someone lifted me off the snow and ice and carried me to the farmhouse which was about a thousand feet from where I landed. This kind person rang the doorbell and held onto me until it opened. From there, I fell onto the kitchen floor.

I awoke in a hospital emergency room. Two police officers were standing nearby. I was in excruciating pain from my head to my feet. A doctor kept asking me questions like, "Do you know where you are? Can you tell me what day it is? Who is the president of the United States?" and other probing questions I might have answered correctly. I just can't recall for sure.

When I asked him if I was going to die, he replied, no. But he told me I was in a terrible car accident, and they were doing their best to fix me up. Hours later, the police were able to question me as I sobered up.

They told me the car I drove flew over a culvert and landed on its roof in a cornfield. If I had my seatbelt on, I would have likely died.

Instead, I was thrown through the windshield before the car smashed to its final resting stop. When I asked about the person who carried me to the farmhouse, the two officers looked at me as if I could still be drunk or maybe crazy. One of the officers replied, "There was no one else, only the elderly couple who live in the farmhouse."

Confused, I added, "Well one of them must have heard or seen my crash and came to get me." He said no, the doorbell woke them, not the crash. This didn't make sense to me.

I wasn't much help to them because I barely remembered anything. My concern shifted from the officers questioning to the person who saved me from the cold frozen ground. I am confident that someone carried me all the way to the farmhouse and rang the doorbell. This person rescued me from death.

Jeez, maybe I was still too drunk to think straight. But I was certain someone saved my life, and I vividly recalled strong arms lifting me up from the ground. The more I thought about this person; my mind veiled him with a glowing force – as if he was a spirit, not a human.

All at once, it hit me, who this person was. God sent an angel to save me. Nothing else made sense. As a final testament to what I came to believe, the officers informed me there was only one set of footprints in the frozen field. And I knew those couldn't have been mine.

Who would ever believe this? After all, I was grossly drunk. In fact, my BAC (blood alcohol level) was .22, more than double the legal limit of .08. I could imagine how people would react if I ever shared this testimony.

At least for a while, I kept my "guardian angel rescue" to myself, so no one would think the crash injured my mind too. It didn't matter if others knew, I knew and it was true. All of the circumstances of that particular early morning led to the same conclusion. It was 4 degrees above zero, with a wind chill of negative 20 degrees Fahrenheit. The crash site was in a desolate area with few farmhouses scattered every couple of miles.

The location of the accident was far away from the house to which I was taken. As I laid unconscious on the cold ground, I should never have been able to wake from that condition. I was bleeding profusely from a bad cut on my face and had suffered a broken back. There is simply no way I would have been able to walk that far under my own power.

Instead of a tragic death, I got a wake-up call. It was a "come-to-Jesus" moment which put my life into proper perspective, yet again. It was God repurposing how I live and reminding me that He had blessed me with a daughter for whom I had promised to love and care for. An untimely and senseless death on such a chilly morning was not in His plans - thankfully, for Kayla's sake.

As I lay there contemplating the incredible gift God had granted me - the gift of a second chance, my family rushed into my hospital room. Knowing that this could have been a far different visit for them (such as a visit to the morgue), I became overwhelmed with emotion. I asked about Kayla and Kelly said she was fine and that she was with Aunt Lynn.

I wanted to hug and squeeze Kayla and tell her how much I loved her. I wanted to tell her I was sorry for being so reckless and jeopardizing our future together.

To my surprise, Shawn entered the room. I couldn't believe he had come to see me. His eyes showed fear as he asked how I felt. I said I would be fine and thanked him for coming. Our eyes locked and we shared a fleeting moment together. No words needed to be said; none were necessary. At that moment, we knew there was something more between us that we hadn't considered seriously yet.

Leaving the hospital days later, I realized my childish reactions to things that don't go my way almost cost me my life. What if I had died in the crash?

CHAPTER ELEVEN

To Have and to Hold

After my wake-up call, I stopped obsessing about Shawn and refocused my energy on Kayla again. I decided to trust God and see what He had in store for us next. Time did not stand still as I waited and hoped for Shawn to be part of our lives. I had to move on.

Kayla was already two years old and mimicking almost everything I did. If I weren't careful, she would become a wild little girl someday, helped by my childish rants and displays of tantrums about her daddy. Second chances mean you get to start over and I intended to do so.

As I was getting more control over my life and my emotions, Shawn tried to figure out what he was going to do with his. He was also soul searching and in a vulnerable state. When his dad encouraged him to join the Army, as he had done a few years before Shawn was born, Shawn agreed. A change of scenery would do him good, he thought. He signed up and soon he would begin Basic Training in Fort Knox, Kentucky. This is the same Army base where his dad served.

Part of me became sad. If we were ever to become anything more, a long distance relationship would only complicate things. But he and I knew that deep down, we both had a lot of growing up to do. If the Army could help him mature, he needed to give it a try.

Before Shawn left, we met at our family house so that he could say goodbye to Kayla. We promised to write to each other, and as I hugged him goodbye, I felt a tug at my heart and didn't want to let go. When we pulled apart, he looked into my eyes and smiled; his beautiful smile still warms my heart today.

As he hugged Kayla, I couldn't help but notice they were standing in the same area where I had conceived her just two years earlier on that careless afternoon in April. Who could have guessed I'd be a parent (not succumbing to abortion again) as a result of that rendezvous? There we were, the three of us; affectionate. And there they were, our parents, watching us as we grow stronger in love. Life is so unpredictable... this is for certain.

Shawn was the first to write. He wrote about how hard boot camp was and how much he missed being home. He wrote that he was making friends and they helped each other get through every challenging day. He also wrote about how much the Army Chaplain helped him when he felt discouraged.

You can imagine the surprise when someone matches all of their numbers to a winning lottery ticket and has to look again - I felt the same as I read how Shawn wanted to be a part of mine and Kayla's life. I didn't know if this meant marriage yet, but I felt it meant something significant. I couldn't get the pen and paper out fast enough to respond.

My return letter told him that I wanted him to be a part of our lives and I gushed that he had always been in my heart.

A week later, I received his reply. He wrote, "*I do love you though I've never admitted it. All I want to do when I get home is run into your arms and hold you all night, safe in my arms. It made me feel good when you told me that you love me too... I can love you right.*"

Being pen pals that summer placed my life in a happy auto-pilot mode. I had control of my actions, but the anticipation of what was to come was guided by each letter I received. I felt our relationship maturing and strengthening with each penned letter.

With each letter, our past sexual indiscretions were becoming a faded memory. I wanted more than sex from Shawn; I wanted to know his hopes and dreams. His letters were giving me a glimpse of his soul, and I prayed I could bear witness to its entirety.

One afternoon when visiting my mom, the phone rang. Mom had gone to fetch something from another room, so I answered it. As I lifted the receiver to my face, I had a feeling it was Shawn. Sure enough, it was. He said he had a feeling I would answer the phone there; he tried dialing my apartment phone, and there was no answer. To his delight, his gut was right.

Shawn's voice seemed edgy as he talked about meaningless happenings on base. I half rolled my eyes wondering why he was telling me about a new Army maneuver he learned earlier in the week. Then he blurted out, "Will you marry me, will you and Kayla move to Colorado with me so we can become a family?"

Just then, my mom re-entered the dining room, and I froze. I had waited so long to hear those words but got scared in her presence.

Could we marry? Were we allowed to get married? I didn't want my worry about our family to make Shawn think I had to give thought to his proposal, so I responded, yes, let's get married! (I'd take care of our family later).

It was July of 1989 and boot camp would be ending in August. I had about a month to get organized and get packing. I floated on cloud nine every day while I scavenged boxes from grocery stores and packed our belongings. Shawn had a few things at our parents' house, so I packed his stuff as well.

Things seemed to be falling into place. Soon we would be embarking on a new journey, taking us away from the place that started us down a path littered with poor decisions. One thousand miles would separate us from the haunted memories that always threatened the joy in my life. Later I would learn that no amount of miles to my old self and my married self would matter in the end.

To our surprise (and relief), our family accepted our marriage plans. I imagine they figured that 'they've been sneaking around for years, why put up a fight?' Sandra even remarked, "It's about time" and gave us all the furniture we needed to fill each room of our new apartment, including a washer and dryer. His mom was very supportive from the start.

The last letter I received from Shawn before completing Basic Training in Kentucky read like poetry, *"...you have been a fixture in my life for so long now...I don't look at our past as a reason for doubt anymore; it acts as a platform for all I feel for you. My love for you is complete, not young and wild, but new and solid."* I must have read his letter at least three times; the words made my heart melt.

Shawn had a few choices of where he could serve, and he chose Fort Carson, Colorado. After boot camp, he had a week of freedom before he'd have to board a plane and check-in at that Army base. Aunt Lynn watched Kayla as I headed out on Interstate 94 in route to Kentucky to bring him home.

By this time I had a new car, a brown 4-door Nissan Sentra equipped to play the 80s songs loaded on cassette tapes I packed for the trip. As I set out for the 8-hour drive, I could barely contain my excitement. I was getting married to the only boy I ever actually loved. Our relationship was no longer a secret.

I reached Fort Knox safely and stopped at the command center to gain access. The soldier on duty found my name, gave me a visitor badge and directions to the Army motel.

When I pulled into the parking lot, I spotted Shawn standing outside the building waiting for me. Getting out of the car, I felt weak in the knees as he stepped over to embrace me. Then he bent to kiss me, and my heart melted. I was utterly in love and couldn't wait to spend the rest of my life with him.

For the remainder of the afternoon, Shawn showed me around the base and introduced me to some of his friends. We ate in the mess hall and then we went back to the motel. Sex was an afterthought that night. For once, it wasn't the purpose of getting together. We talked about Kayla and moving to Colorado. I brought my favorite beer; Michelob Dry (at the time), and we drank it and enjoyed simply being together.

There was a different vibe between us; instead of a sexual hunger, it felt surreal knowing our time spent together wasn't ending soon, or in the morning. I felt our past teenage ambitions far differed from the ones on which we were about to embark.

In the morning, we loaded Shawn's things in the trunk of my car and headed back home to Wisconsin. We left later than I wanted, but we finally got on the road by 11:00 am. The drive took longer going back than when I came because of a horrific traffic accident. We stood still on the interstate for hours because a semi-truck hauling new vehicles lost control of the harnesses which kept them secure. The cars on the top layer flipped over onto passing cars and smashed them and those within, like pancakes.

Images of the presumed victims under the heaps of metal haunted me for years. I could not comprehend how such a tragedy could happen and it sobered our mood for most of the drive. It saddened us that people died on the interstate that day in such a vulgar way. If we left earlier like I had wanted to, it could have been us.

For the next week, we were practically inseparable. Sharing a cart at the grocery store and making a choice of what cut of meat to purchase, offered me a sense of comfort – a glimpse of normal behavior for couples. Instead of devising a time and a place for sex, we were shopping for food and making meals together while Kayla played at our feet.

It felt odd at first to openly display our love for each other, particularly in front of our family. No one seemed to be bothered, so eventually, I let go of such worry.

The day Shawn had to report for duty came fast. We couldn't fly with him to Colorado because someone had to get our belongings on a moving truck. And because we couldn't afford a moving company, I volunteered to haul our possessions across three state lines.

It was a muggy August afternoon as Shawn packed up the few items he needed to take with him. He wore his Army Service Uniform and as he swung the heavy green jacket around his back and loaded his arms in each sleeve, he looked like he was in a pressure cooker because of the suppressive heat in the apartment (there was no air conditioning). In contrast, I wore a tank top and jean shorts as we anxiously drove to the airport. Neither of us wanted to be separated, even for one day.

A few days later, our family helped load our stuff onto the U-Haul that would string my car on a trailer behind. Out of nowhere, unasked questions abruptly tried to corrupt my mind, like, "Was I making the right decision moving so far away? How would I survive not being able to visit mom every day? Since moving back home, Kayla saw my mom almost every day, how would she feel about not being able to spend time with grandma?"

The panic was short-lived as my brother David gave the thumbs-up after checking the tires, mirrors, breaks, locks, and anything else which could cause me trouble. We said our goodbyes, and with tear-rimmed eyes, I hugged my mom. I bravely told her not to worry and that I would use the calling card she gave to me to let her know when we safely arrived in Colorado.

At the age of 22, I sat in the driver's seat of a moving truck with Kayla strapped next to me. For a fleeting moment, I became afraid of driving such a big vehicle. I must have looked so small and silly, all 110 pounds of me sitting on a wide blue leather seat stretched to the passenger side where my even smaller daughter sat. I remember thinking that a few 300-pound men could easily fit in that space.

What did I know about driving a truck with a trailer? One thousand miles seemed almost impossible to trek alone with a two-year-old. Nevertheless, love gives you the courage to do things you never thought possible, and I daringly pushed the pedal down and began the journey to a new life.

The trip was fine until we made a stop in Nebraska for gas and a bathroom break. The maneuvers and concentration it took to switch lanes when cars were driving too slow, took a toll on my nerves. I had to keep remembering there was a trailer on the back-end and every move I made, I had to consider that extra length.

When we reached the Nebraska stop, I was more distracted than I should have been with the loads of responsibility I had on my shoulders. As I parked alongside the gas pump, I paused and took a deep breath to get rid of the toxic stress that lingered from the off-ramp and into the gas station with me.

Sick of the air conditioning, I rolled down the windows and told Kayla to sit tight. I filled the gas tank and then unstrapped her, and we went inside to pay. By the time we got to the counter, I realized that I had left my purse on the front seat of the truck. As we raced back to the truck, I had a sinking feeling in the pit of my stomach.

With the windows rolled down, it was easy to grab my purse without opening the door. So it was for a thief too. When I reached in to get my wallet, I knew the money was gone because the bulge from all the cash I withdrew from my bank account was gone. All of it, every penny.

The thief was kind enough to leave my driver's license and eyeglasses. The bank I belonged to back home was not a national chain, so I closed it and planned to open a new one with Shawn when we got settled. I had no ATM card or any checks, all the cash I owned was now gone.

Panic filled me immediately as I started to tremble in fear. What now? I took gasoline and had no way to pay for it. We weren't even close to our destination - we still had at least 400 miles to reach the Army base. We would need at least two more tanks of gas. Red-faced and teary eyed, I held Kayla close and walked back to talk with the store manager. He was an older gentleman and thankfully, very understanding and helpful.

First, he asked if I wanted to file a police report and I said no. Chances of catching whoever stole my money were nil because the gas station had no video cameras. I was certain the thief was long gone and gleefully driving down the interstate devising ways to spend my cash.

Then the manager informed me he could help facilitate a Western Union Money Transfer. He explained how it worked, and I tried calling my mom. If she could get to a Western Union location back home, she could wire me some money. I didn't want all that was stolen, just enough to make it to Colorado. There was no answer at home.

Then I called Aunt Lynn, and luckily, she answered. I don't know how she understood what

I was saying because I was crying so hard, but she got it and asked to talk to the manager.

Soon the wire transfer was in process, but it would take hours for it to be complete. In those days, it wasn't as easy as using a credit or debit card to send money to someone. One had to go to a Western Union office and give cash and of course, pay a hefty fee. The amount of time it took didn't matter to me, being rescued did. Once again, my aunt and uncle were there for me when I needed desperate help. They really are awesome like that.

Kayla and I patiently sat on a fly infested picnic table off to the side of the building. We ate sandwiches my mom had made for our trip, and as I watched the people coming and going from the gas hose to the store, Kayla colored in a book. Earlier I tried calling Shawn to tell him what had happened so that he wouldn't worry when we didn't show up as expected, but I couldn't reach him. So, I left a message with his commanding officer.

When dusk settled in, I started to worry about our safety, so we went back inside the store. The manager said he was just coming to find us because the transfer was complete. Wow, what a relief I thought. As he counted the cash into my hand, I thanked him for all his help. He smiled and said he has a daughter about the same age as me and I reminded him of her. I paid him for the gas, and with a grateful heart, we headed back to the interstate.

The whole ordeal cost us four hours of travel time. It was nearly bedtime for me, but I could not afford to spend one penny on a hotel room. Driving straight through was our only option, so I popped open a Pepsi and told Kayla it was sleep time. I drove in silence because I didn't want the radio to keep her up.

The air was crisp and fresh at that time, so I rolled down my window halfway. With only the sound of the wind pulsating at my left ear, my mind drifted to the hours of our journey. Earlier on the phone, Aunt Lynn had said, "It could have been worse, it's only money." I knew what she meant; there could have been a kidnapping, or we could have been in a wreck. I was coming around to this way of thinking - things can always be worse. Later in my life, this would become one of my mantras.

By the grace of God, we made it safely to Colorado Springs with no further ado. It was Sunday, so Shawn was not working. I stopped at the command center, offered my name, and received a campus map. The officer circled my destination and wished me a pleasant day.

Shawn was staying in the barracks for the time being, living his last days as a single man. When I found the right building, I pulled in and found him motioning where I should park the truck and trailer. As soon as the engine shut off, I jumped out, and we hugged. His embrace felt incredible and safe. Kayla yelled, "What about me?" and he went and unstrapped her and hugged her too.

While gazing at the majestic mountains and bluest sky I'd ever seen, the word "wow" quietly escaped my lips. Shawn said, "I know, isn't it beautiful?" Then he moved my body slightly to the left and pointed to a spot nestled in a mountain and told me "that is NORAD" (North American Aerospace Defense Command). I was unimpressed because I didn't know what that meant. When he said, "It is a top secret place that provides air protection for North America," then I was in awe.

As I stood there with Shawn's arm around my shoulder, I felt all the anxiety from the long drive fall away. I couldn't wait to get started with my new life.

We married on Friday, October 13, 1989, at the Colorado Springs courthouse by a justice of the peace. We thought, for a split second, that getting married on such an infamous date would be bad luck. Then we giggled because our wedding day had nothing to do with luck. It had everything to do with fate.

In a wood-paneled courtroom with flat mauve carpeting at our feet and with Kayla by our side, we exchanged vows, rings, and a kiss to seal our commitment. It was short and sweet. We wished our family had been with us, but we made a promise to renew our vows and celebrate after we moved back home.

On that day, we changed the course of history. We believed we could defy the odds, unlike our parents, and survive what we knew could come our way. Difficulties, challenges, heartbreak, and tears. We would tackle them together because we were meant to be; it was destiny.

CHAPTER TWELVE

Between Us

After we officially tied the knot, we got right into married life. Although Shawn had lived with his ex-wife for a short period and had already experienced intimately living with the opposite sex, I had no experience. I'm a neat freak and cannot tolerate a mess. It isn't that he's a slob, but he didn't do things like hang up his towel after a shower (at least not at first).

Money was a problem right out of the gate. I had enjoyed being independent and free to use my money how and when I wanted. Now I was unemployed. It's no secret that Army wages are enormously insufficient. Lack of financial freedom and stability added stress to our marriage on a regular basis.

The idea of putting Kayla in daycare was unthinkable to us, so I found waitressing work at night. As Shawn came home from work, I left. In the beginning, we didn't see much of each other, but eating and paying bills took precedence.

Living far away from home added to my daily struggles. Long distance phone calls were expensive, so I couldn't call my mom as often as I wanted. If I were back home, I could easily drive over for a visit or call basically for free. Now I had a barrier to reach the one person I needed in times of conflict.

At the age of 22 and 20, we had a lot to learn about adulthood. We tried to be mature and act like grown-ups for the sake of Kayla, but we also desired the footloose and fancy-free fun our single friends were enjoying. We went through a stint of going with them to a popular nightclub on Saturday nights.

Although it was fun to get out and let loose on the dance floor, I drank too much beer. Just like in my teen years, too much alcohol transformed me into "lively Laura," and this made Shawn uncomfortable - most especially since other young Army men found my "lively" side quite appealing despite having a gold band wrapped around my left ring finger.

I got pulled onto the dance floor many times by handsome young men we didn't know. One night after too many of these bold tactics, Shawn pulled me off the illuminated floor and out to the dim lit parking lot.

A fight ensued. I couldn't understand why he was so angry; I was only dancing with those men. And we weren't even touching each other; I reserved the slow dances for him. As rain lightly fell upon us, he lectured me that men can perceive my willingness to dance with them as an invitation to something more. I replied he was crazy, that my behavior was innocent.

Like a ping pong match, we went back and forth for a few minutes until my temper reached a boiling point. With hot angry tears, I yanked my wedding ring off, tossed it far enough to make a point, but close enough (hopefully) for Shawn to find it and then I stormed back into the club.

Thankfully, he had the sense to retrieve the ring, and then retrieve me from inside the club. Shawn didn't drink much in those days; probably because of his grueling Army schedule (he had to be on the Army base by 5:00 am for physical training, Monday through Friday). I, on the other hand, didn't know when to stop once I got started.

When Shawn came back inside, he found me on the dance floor with another man. I didn't care what he thought; I felt hurt from his jealous rant. As "U Can't Touch This" by MC Hammer blared, he grabbed me by the arm and tried to pull me off the floor. Without my wedding ring on, my dancing partner didn't know I was hitched and tried to stop him.

That was a mistake. Shawn turned toward him and yelled, "This is my wife, if you don't get your f*****g hands off her, I will destroy you." When his hands dropped down, Shawn took my arm and led me out of the club. We didn't speak a word on the drive home. After I brushed my teeth and got ready to plop into bed, I saw my wedding ring on my pillow.

Shawn was already in bed, facing the opposite way and pretending to be asleep. I snuggled up next to him and softly said I was sorry for acting crazy. I winced at the thought my wedding ring could have been gone forever.

On Shawn's furlough after Basic Training, we had gone on a date in downtown Milwaukee and ended up at a favorite Mall. I had built up good credit, and we applied for financing at one of those jewelry stores that took up shop like a corner house on a city block. Together, we picked out our wedding bands. After we had eaten lunch at the food court on the third floor, Shawn asked me to step outside on the balcony.

To my surprise, he got down on bended knee and officially asked me to marry him with the ring I just picked out. It was a warm and breezy afternoon, and a handful of people sat nearby, some sipping fruity beverages, a new craze at the time. When I said, "Yes" clapping arose and added to the awareness that our engagement was real now. I was engaged to be married.

Losing my wedding ring in a puddled parking lot of a club would have crushed my spirit. When Shawn turned around to face me in bed, he said he didn't want to go to clubs anymore. I agreed.

After that night, we stopped going out and realized that we could stay home and have more fun with our friends (single or married). It was cheaper, no babysitting fees, and the beer was less expensive when we bought it from the Army base.

Unless Shawn was "down-range," he worked Monday – Friday. I despised "down-range" because this was when his unit went south to Pinõn Canyon, an Army Maneuver Site for field training. These excursions were no shorter than two weeks, and I grew to dislike sleeping alone. I finally got accustomed to the rhythms of married life. I did the dishes, Shawn prepared the meals. I did the laundry, he took out the trash. When the car needed an oil change, Shawn took care of it. When Kayla needed to go to the doctor, I took care of it. When he was "down-range" – I did everything.

We made good friends while in the Army; most were in the same boat we were. Poor. A bunch of us would donate plasma on Saturday mornings. In those days, $15.00 for a donation went a long away at the PX (Post Exchange – store selling cheap consumer goods & services exclusive to Army patrons). I didn't enjoy giving plasma; I typically got light headed and woozy. Once when I passed out cold, I never donated again. Embarrassed, I reasoned no amount of money is worth losing consciousness in a room full of strangers.

Most of our friends were single. We had a few married-couple friends; one, in particular, we became very close with. Erik and Shawn were in the same battalion and when they'd go "downrange," sometimes we girls would take turns bunking at each other's places. Kim became a good friend and eventually, a cherished confidant. The four of us are still good friends today.

Our friendships were critical when our marriage became rocky at times. The ever-present elephant in the room was the baggage we brought into our marriage. We never talked about our teenage years and the struggles we endured when I got pregnant and had the abortions. We never discussed how we felt when our parents split us apart. By that time, it seemed hardly worth it. Let bygones be bygones, I reasoned.

The mind doesn't always forget and move on as we wish it would. We piled up too many occasions to keep it at bay for long. Too much was unresolved. We had caused a lot of chaos; not only within our own lives but in our family. We perpetrated lies and hurts that could never be taken back. Before saying "I do," we should have gone to counseling and started our marriage with a clean slate. Because we didn't, all of our past sat lurking on a shelf, waiting to rear its ugly head.

Meanwhile, we attended church every Sunday. Worship gave us the perception that we could move on from our past and be present by establishing a solid religious foundation for

Kayla. Putting the focus on Kayla's religious rearing was a good distraction.

There is something to be said about worship, especially when done with the people you love. From finding the right pew bench to sit, to smiling when you find that one of your favorites hymns made the cut that week, to offering peace to fellow Catholics and then receiving Holy Eucharist with the reassurance that you are not alone in daily struggles; Mass is a sacred ritual for a heart in any condition.

Around this time, we started talking about having another baby. Once I stopped swallowing my birth control pills, it didn't take long to get pregnant. Though when I got this news, I had an uneasy feeling. I didn't tell Shawn how I felt and hoped it was just that my hormones were off balance.

Sitting in the doctor's office, Shawn and I waited patiently for an ultrasound in my fourth month of pregnancy. I was excited to share this experience with him as he wasn't present for Kayla's ultrasound. The baby had shown signs of life every so often with a flutter, but as we waited, I couldn't recall the last time I felt one.

As the doctor scanned my belly, she paused and moved her eyes closer to the screen. She moved the wand around a bit more and after a few minutes stopped. She turned her body towards us and said, "I am so sorry." She could not find a baby. My bad feeling proved to be a miscarriage. Shawn took my hand and squeezed it and said he was sorry too.

When I looked over at him, tears filled his eyes. I was too numb to cry and simply got ready for what came next. The doctor informed us I would need to have a minor procedure done right away. She called it a D&C, which stands for Dilation and Curettage. In a nutshell, it's a procedure which dilates the cervix so that the uterus can be scraped to remove any remaining pregnancy tissue. After this, I needed to lay low and rest to avert cramping and bleeding.

Sound familiar? It did for me; it was a perfect eidetic vision. It was the same procedure done years before, better known to me as an abortion. As I laid back once again, memories of years past came flooding in. But this time I wasn't at Planned Parenthood, I was at the Air Force Academy. And I wasn't being cared for by a cold-hearted doctor who didn't speak a word to me, my present doctor was an OB-GYN, and she was warm and kind.

My mind was unstoppable as I began a painful trip down memory lane. Trying to halt further recollection, I reminded myself I miscarried this time, I wasn't having an abortion. And this time, I was married and Shawn and I wanted to have a baby. We were trying to have a baby. We were ready to have another baby.

Was I being punished now, after all these years? My thoughts took me all over the place and couldn't land anywhere helpful. The D&C brought back too much pain, and all I wanted to do was crawl in bed and hit rewind and erase.

On our way back home, I sat in the passenger's seat with the same numb feeling I had when dad drove me home after my second abortion. If Shawn was talking to me, I did not hear one word. I didn't even notice we had stopped to pick up Kayla from a friend's house. The next thing I can recall is laying in bed and feeling so empty inside. I feared we would never have another child.

Maybe Kayla would be our only child. Sadly, I thought about her not having any siblings. Of course, she could've had two already. Like a song you can't get out of your head when you want to move on and sing something different, I couldn't get past the thoughts of my abortions. I thought she could have had two already, had I not aborted them earlier in my life.

Shawn tried to be level headed and said we'd try again. He even brought God into the fold by telling me everything happens for a reason. I rolled my eyes and half-heartedly agreed. I didn't have the emotional strength to resist such logic.

What I needed was a distraction, something which could take my mind off of losing my baby. I got one, a visit from our parents. They called to tell us they wanted to fly out for a week. A visit from our parents made us all happy and was the perfect medicine for the emotional sickness which evaded our moods.

We picked them up at the Denver airport with Kayla beside herself with excitement. Shawn proudly showed them the Army base, and it was evident by the look on Allan's face, the pride he felt for Shawn, the soldier. The weather was perfect as we took them to Pike's Peak and over to the Garden of the Gods Nature Center.

It felt great to be accepted as a married couple and as a family. It was a significant milestone to share our new life without the distractions of our past. The visit was exactly what I needed, and I didn't want it to end. It was hard to say goodbye, but I felt a renewed spirit as we waved them onto their return flight.

A few months later, I was pregnant again. Once I surpassed my fourth month, I felt a little more confident that this pregnancy would go full-term. At five months, I had another ultrasound. With Shawn by my side, the doctor used her magic wand to scan over my growing belly. On the computer screen, we saw a lively baby, and we heard the heartbeat loud and vigorous.

When the doctor asked if we wanted to know the sex, we said sure. It was more of an economic decision than anything else, as we were still poor. We had plenty of girl things, the opposite sex would require us to budget for boy things.

The doctor pointed to our baby's penis on the screen and said we are having a boy. Having a boy was music to our ears. Now we would have one of each. I asked if there was a chance I could lose this baby now. Every day I feared I could, and I couldn't stand the uneasiness, it afflicted on my soul. She said nothing was a guarantee; however, all indications from the ultrasound showed he was a strong and healthy baby.

Shawn took great care of me during the pregnancy. He joined me at Lamaze class and raced to King Soopers grocery store when I had sporadic cravings that I couldn't shake. He rubbed my back, talked to our baby at bedtime, and let me sleep in on the weekends. I soaked up all his helpfulness this time around.

As Christmas approached, Shawn had 13 days of leave saved, and we cashed them all in to drive home to Wisconsin. Still poor, we drove twenty-four hours straight through to avoid hotel expense. As Shawn shifted the car to park, I sat frozen in the driveway of our family home. I became anxious; the last time I was here, I was a single woman. Now I was married to my stepbrother and pregnant once again. Our parents accepted this reality, but I wasn't sold that *all* of our siblings had.

It turns out that our family had moved past our past. Everyone was busy building their lives and had no time to question or be concerned about my marriage to Shawn. We ended up enjoying our visit immensely. Kayla especially had a fantastic time, as she was the only grandchild at the time and was showered with attention and enough gifts for ten little girls.

Our visit flew by, and soon we were jammed into our Nissan Sentra with Kayla barely able to sit comfortably in her spot behind Shawn. My mom had gathered baby boy items from various family and in addition to the generous Christmas gifts we received, we were at capacity. We drove straight through back to Colorado with peace in our hearts from such a wonderful time with our family.

Our son's due date was May 1st; however, on the eve of April 23rd, I went into labor after Shawn and I had gone to bed. Earlier in the day, I'd had a spark of energy and cleaned the entire kitchen from ceiling to floor. High energy gushes are sometimes called nesting, and it should have been a warning that labor was on the horizon, but I either didn't recognize it, or I ignored it.

At around 11:30 pm, I nudged Shawn and told him I was having contractions. He jumped up and asked how far apart. I wasn't timing them but said this is it. We sat in bed for a bit longer to see if another contraction came. Another one came, along with my water breaking. Shawn jumped out of bed and called our friend who'd be watching Kayla during the hospital stay. Like a flash, we were out the door.

At the time, Shawn did not have a valid driver's license. It had been revoked back in Wisconsin for habitual speeding. We were taking a chance with him driving at that time of night, but we didn't have much choice, my contractions were getting stronger and more frequent.

As luck would have it, as we sped toward the hospital on the Air Force Academy grounds, we saw police lights behind us, signaling for us to pull over. Shawn was most definitely guilty of speeding, but we didn't have time for a traffic stop. As the officer approached the vehicle,

Shawn yelled back, "My wife is in labor!" When the officer saw my big belly, he said excitedly, "Follow me!" and off we sped to the hospital entrance.

Instead of Shawn getting in trouble for driving with a revoked license, we were escorted all the way to the hospital. Once we parked in front of the emergency room, the officer ran inside, grabbed a wheelchair, gently seated me, and wheeled me inside. He shook Shawn's hand and said congratulations, and that was the last time we ever saw him.

Whew! What a relief for once, bad luck didn't ensue. Labor went fast, and Shawn did his best to keep me calm and help with my breathing. He put his Lamaze coach hat on, but at one point during a painful contraction, I made a strange moaning noise, and inexplicably Shawn laughed. As he leaned in, inches away from my painstaking face, he asked how I was doing. I thought, What the hell kind of question is this? How does it look like I'm doing? Agitated, I swung my fist to his jaw and asked him how he was doing. I apologized but didn't feel sorry as the next, stronger contraction consumed my body.

Keenan was born a few hours later, and I cried happy tears as Shawn cut the cord and placed him on my sweaty chest. As with Kayla's birth, after he was born, all the labor pain was already a forgotten memory. As we both watched him take his first breath and kick start his lungs with some good cries, I took pause and thanked God for a successful pregnancy and a healthy baby boy.

A few hours later, our friend brought Kayla to the hospital to meet her brother. She was so excited, yet gentle when she held him for the first time. I knew she was going to be a great big sister and it warmed my heart she had a sibling now.

Shawn took care of letting our family know about Keenan's birth. From all accounts, they were congratulatory and happy that the baby and I were healthy. The next day, we went home to begin another new chapter of our lives together. We were now a family of four. God blessed us again, and I should have understood that Keenan's birth negated my past sins, like Kayla's birth had. At least for the moment, I relished in our blessings and was grateful.

Having a newborn in our family made our lives busy. Kayla helped with feeding her brother and always made sure he had his pacifier when he got fussy. Shawn worked during the day as I took care of the kids, and at night he took care of them as I earned extra money waitressing. We went to church, read books together, and ate dinner as a family. On most accounts, we were a typical family.

We still had those underlying issues from our past we put off resolving. It prevented us from being released from the guilt and shame we still harbored deep within. The consequence would show at times when we had a disagreement about something trivial, and it would turn into the sky falling. We had a hard time figuring out why we couldn't get through an argument without throwing something from our past at each other.

Two months after Keenan was born, we made plans to have him Baptized in our church back home. Shawn had ten days of leave saved, and we drove straight through again.

The night before Keenan's baptism, my mom watched the kids while Shawn and I went out for drinks with our siblings and a few close friends. The next morning, I had a tinge of a headache from drinking too much beer, but the words Father spoke during the ceremony were loud and clear. Baptism is not just an event that ends when we leave the church; it is a lifelong commitment with God.

As I glanced around at those who joined us that morning, my heart became filled with happiness. My grandpa and grandma were present. Of all the people in that church, it was them I was most grateful for being there. They walked the walk and talked the talk when it came to their commitment to God. My grandparents were "old-school" Catholics; following the doctrine to a tee. I wanted to make them proud of me; I wanted to emulate the same commitment to the church as they had.

For the most part, Shawn and I were doing okay in this regard. We went to church every Sunday. But we didn't go to confession, and we did not attend other Catholic Holy Days of Obligation. We also didn't tithe the right amount; we couldn't afford to. I guess we can be called "new-school" Catholics; we picked and chose what part of the doctrine we wanted to follow.

The ceremony went well; it was a private one held after Mass. The remainder of Shawn's leave went fast, and as we drove back to Colorado, my heart longed to be home again. I missed my family and friends. I wanted to see them more than just a couple of times a year.

From the start of Shawn's enlistment, he knew he wasn't in it for the long haul. After his four-year commitment, he would not re-enlist. By his third year, though, the Army was reducing their troop levels nationwide, and offering lower ranking soldiers an early release. We jumped at the chance to get out of the Army a year early and move back home.

By December of 1991, all the paperwork was in order as we loaded another U-Haul and headed back home to Wisconsin. It was hard to say goodbye to the friends we made, but we all promised to stay in touch and visit when we could. With our children strapped in-between us, we headed out to begin yet another new chapter together.

CHAPTER THIRTEEN

50 Miles North

Government red tape prevented us from getting an apartment ahead of time. We were informed by a bun-haired stout lady in the personnel office that it would take several weeks to receive Shawn's final paycheck. She did give us good news when she handed us a travel payment. At least we could rent a U-Haul and get back home. This time we had a bank account with a national chain, so we kept what little cash we had safely in the bank. Being poor stunk to high heaven.

Ideally, we hoped to move in with our parents short-term. However, Allan had recently accepted a job promotion which took him and my mom to Indiana. Aunt Lynn and Uncle Ryan could be counted on again to take us in and provide cover for us until the money came.

All of our furniture and most of our belongings moved into a storage unit, only to haul it all back out two months later when the money arrived in the mail. Shawn found work at a factory in our hometown. We moved into a small two-bedroom apartment on the same street with a large park and baseball diamond. Remarkably, our new place was the same one Shawn lived in when he was a little boy after his dad first got out of the Army. Could this be a sign? (we wondered).

Six months after moving in, we moved out and into a single family house rental with Erik and Kim, our good friends from the Army. Erik took a job in the area, and they moved from Pennsylvania. Since both of our families were struggling financially, we decided to share the burden and room together.

Kim had given birth to a baby boy one month after Keenan was born and had a daughter the same age as Kayla. The kids all got along great. We adults did too, at first. After a while, I started to feel boxed in with little privacy and felt we never had enough time alone as an independent family. I began to get agitated by small things that surely should not have meant anything. I dreamed of having our own place again and Erik and Kim living at a different address.

After months of trying to make it work, Erik and Kim moved back for a different job opportunity. The lease ran out, and we could not afford the payment on our own. Shawn's "everything happens for a reason" mantra kicked in when we got a call from his mom. Sandra's husband, Bob, had a job opportunity for Shawn at the car dealership where he worked. They lived 50 miles north, and since we had nothing to lose, we jumped at another new beginning.

Shawn hated his factory job, and we had no place to live at the end of the month. The city, 50 miles north, was in-between a large city and small town, which we thought was perfect for raising a family.

The very next weekend, we drove up to investigate what could be our new hometown.

Sandra was our tour guide, and as we drove around the city, we felt a good vibe. She took us to a huge park located on the shores of Lake Winnebago, and I envisioned us picnicking and feeding the animals at the petting zoo located right across from the playground. I spotted a waterfall near some paddle boats and remarked what a lovely park it was.

Sandra and Bob lived in a townhouse complex that offered two bedroom units with an upstairs and basement - like a mini house. It so happened that the townhouse right next to them was vacant and waiting for a family like us to move in. The complex even had a playground and swimming pool in the courtyard.

Everything felt right, so Shawn went back on Monday morning to interview for the job. He called from Sandra's place to tell me he'd gotten the job and I exploded with praise. I immediately started to plan the move, and within a couple of weeks, we settled in our new place.

Shawn and I were delighted to discover a solid Catholic Church and school presence. There were five Catholic Churches and three schools, to be exact. We became members of one of them and enrolled Kayla in time to attend first grade.

It didn't take long before we made new friends. The kids loved our new townhouse, and I enjoyed listening to their heightened squeals as they jumped into the pool with inflatable rings around their arms. Most times, I lounged next to the edge of the water so that I could leap in when my skin needed a break from the heat. I'd splash around with the kids for a bit and then get out to let the sun warm my tanned body again.

Taking Kayla to school on her first day brought nostalgia and pride at the same time. Although my days in Catholic grade school were tainted with too many pranks, I had nothing but good memories. As I let go of her hand and wished her great things, tears trickled from the corner of my eyes. Only a few tears, but enough to make me understand the importance of being a parent. It hurt to let go.

My dad called one day and asked if Shawn and I wanted to fly to Florida as a gift from him and Paula. A late wedding gift for us and the honeymoon we never took. I ecstatically said yes. Sandra watched the kids, and soon we were coasting like free birds on a no-kid get-a-way.

It was late August and steamy hot. Paula and my dad lived in a house on a channel that led to the Gulf of Mexico. Dad was a fisherman at heart and had a big boat and all the gear needed to scoop up dinner on a daily basis. Shawn was enamored with dad's nautical skills and mimicked his every move as we floated on the Gulf and reeled in the daily catch.

Dad woke us at the crack of dawn, citing the early bird gets the worm motivation. I was an early riser too and enjoyed sharing a hot cup of coffee with him before the sun made the air thick enough to cut through. Shawn could barely contain his excitement. This was the day we'd be in the Gulf for an extended fishing expedition. Paula had to work, so it was only three of us.

Quietly we inched our way up the channel, as dad did not want to make loud engine noises and wake residents that didn't care if the bird got the worm early. The motor purred softly as I remarked how peaceful it was that morning. As we approached the opening to the Gulf, dad stood and pushed the throttle forward giving us more speed.

Like driving through a dark tunnel in daylight hours, we emerged on the other side to the open sky saying good morning. Our eyes adjusted to what looked like orange juice and lemonade spilling over from Heaven and staining the backdrop above. No one said a word; we were too captivated by the beauty before us.

As we glided along, I felt intimidated by the vast amount of water surrounding the boat. There were a few other eager beavers out for the catch that morning as well. With no land in sight for miles, their presence took away the isolation I felt. If the waters swallowed us, we could be saved by them, I reasoned.

When dad had us positioned in what he called, *a hot zone*, we dropped lines and waited with anticipation for the tug. For the next several hours, we reeled in some keepers and some we tossed back for being too tiny. When we had enough fish for several meals (and people), we tucked the rods away and began our journey back to land.

Then the storm came. In the hours we were at sea, the sky progressed from orange juice and lemonade to bright baby blue to dark and angry. Though the dark and angry sky was behind us and the bright baby blue before us, I feared getting caught in a storm. Dad reassured me it was heading toward Cuba, the opposite direction. But he was wrong.

In less than an hour, the storm was upon us, and suddenly we were in trouble. I took cover in the belly of the boat. Dad was barking out orders to Shawn while I was tossing up my peanut butter and jelly sandwich in a toilet below. We were in the teeth of a tropical gale which was not mentioned in the morning forecast and the boat all but capsized from the hurling waves.

As the boat began to normalize, I was still green with sea sickness. The waves leveled out; the storm subsided, so I opened the hatch and climbed on the deck. Shawn looked as though a shark had chased him; although he'd gotten sunburned the day before, his skin was as white as Casper the Friendly Ghost. Dad looked a bit shaken as well. Neither one of them had words to speak, so I took a seat and thanked God for getting us through the squall, and for my dad's seaman skills.

Being survivors is what we'd consider ourselves now. Add a few "what ifs" and you can surmise where we were in our mental state. Seeing land gained me some composure. I spotted Paula waving her arms high as we got closer to shore. She must've heard about the storm and left work to make sure we were safe.

As I jumped off onto the pier, my legs were like jelly; it took a few minutes to get my land legs back. As we headed back to the house, I sighed in relief as dad grabbed our dinner catches, Shawn lugged the cooler, and I got everything else. I knew what would come next... libations, steady and strong.

The remaining vacation time flew. Soon we were back in the sky on our journey home. Overall we had a remarkable time, and I was grateful for the hospitality and generosity of Dad and Paula. Though now, I looked forward to hugging my kids and giving them the cheesy trinkets we bought at souvenir shops along the beach. Nothing like a week away from daily aggravations to renew my outlook. I felt energized as we retrieved our kids from Sandra and Bob's place. Being home was marvelous.

My rejuvenated energy prompted me to consider going to college. I wanted to be able to take our kids on vacations like the one Shawn and I were just on, and waitressing wasn't going to give us such opportunity. I wanted a career which earned me a decent salary. I hated being poor.

While cooking eggs one Sunday morning after church, I presented the topic to Shawn. He was preoccupied at the helm of the stove burner because each of us enjoyed our eggs made differently and he wanted to get them done to our liking.

With money always at the forefront, he asked how we could pay for it. I suggested I might qualify for financial aid. He shrugged his shoulders as he plopped the scrambled eggs on my plate and said, "It doesn't hurt to find out." So I did, the next day.

Nine years had passed since I last thought about textbooks and homework. I knew I wasn't cut out for the big league, the University, so I drove to the community college instead. As I found my way to the Admissions Office, I noticed how much older I was than the students roaming the halls. I thought maybe I was too old to pursue this now. Perhaps I missed my mark when I neglected to learn in my high school years.

As I turned to retreat, a woman walking toward me with glasses perched on the end of her nose asked if she could help me. As she got closer, she removed her glasses and let them fall to her chest, secured by a fancy beaded chain holder. I confessed I wanted to enroll in a program, but I had no idea how to get it done. She smiled and said follow me and led me to the correct office.

She asked my first name and introduced me to a youngster, no more than 20 years old, sitting at a desk. As she turned to leave, she said so-and-so would be able to get me what I needed to get started. She wished me luck and said she hoped to see me again. So-and-so prodded and poked around my hopes and dreams to determine the Supervisory/Management program suited me the best.

Going to college was the one time in which being poor did well by us, as I received grant money from the federal government to kick-off my new pursuit. Snuggled next to Shawn one night before bed, I envisioned the proud moment of shaking the Dean's hand as he gave me my hard-earned diploma. I would ward off the low-ball employment offers to accept the lavish six-figure corporate job, giving me a corner office overlooking the park side of the building, not a parking lot.

Yeah, I could see this happening like winning the lottery. My confidence suffered a blow when my adviser told me I had to pass remedial math and English classes before enrolling in the "real" ones earning me credits toward a degree. So I was stupid? Shawn assured me I was not and encouraged me to stay the course and study hard. He is one of those irritating people who never has to spend much time grasping a concept. He has a brilliant mind, and I credit his encouragement and insights for much of the success in my early college years.

Trying to make up for lost time, I took on 15 credits the first semester. My advisor "advised" me not to, but I told her I didn't want to be in school forever. Between homework, waitressing, and my family, my plate was overflowing. My temper got short and little things which shouldn't have bothered me did. Shawn and I started fighting more often. The arguments had a tendency to turn into an all-out "throwing knives" kind of fighting.

Most often we referenced our teenage years. I tossed in remarks about him not being there for me when I tortured through the abortions, and he returned folly by explaining he would have preferred to be with me than living in our dysfunctional family house. Our bickering never resolved anything and only added tension and frustration to our marriage.

After a few months of on and off again fighting, I lost it, and after one bad fight, I gathered some of Shawn's clothing and threw them out through the window from our second-story bedroom. Both our kids witnessed this one, and I felt ashamed and embarrassed. I wailed to Shawn that I did not want our marriage to fall into the same fate as our parents. We had to get control.

The ghosts of my past were out of the cage and making up for lost time. Since marrying Shawn a few years earlier, I did my best to keep their evil spirits away, but their forces were stronger than my overloaded capacity as a wife, mom, and student at the time could handle. One's enemy is most successful when weakness prevails in the soul.

The only thing holding together our family was our commitment to church and God. Every Sunday we'd attend Mass and worship together as a family. We made Church, God, and prayer a priority. We prayed at mealtime and bedtime. We taught our kids that God should be at the center of all we think about, act upon and speak. Our pure intentions helped keep our marriage together. It wasn't always happy, but we never talked about divorce.

At one Sunday Mass, I learned about a marriage retreat scheduled a few weeks later. The church bulletin encouraged all married couples to attend, whether married for one year or twenty. You'd check-in on Friday night and then be dismissed after Sunday Mass. The program promised to bring us closer together and make our marriage stronger. The announcement touted tools and resources which would help us "fight fair" and learn to appreciate our differences. Just what we needed, I thought.

Shawn never read the bulletins, so as we walked home, I told him what I had read. Setting the scene in my head, I placed us in front of a fireplace, with a nice glass of wine in hand while we relaxed on a loveseat learning how to love each other more significantly. I was convinced, was he? To my delight, he said yes.

We dropped our kids with family and excitedly set out to rekindle our love. After seven years of marriage, who couldn't use a renewal? The retreat was in an old convent on the property of a Catholic High School. What appeared to be married couples greeted us warmly upon arrival. Their smiles were a sign of encouragement as we were escorted to our sleeping quarters to drop off our things.

Our room reminded me of the dorms I once stayed in when I visited Marquette University as a young girl for the big sister program. The room, no larger than 10 x 10 was stuffy from the daylight sun, and it felt like the windows had remained shut since the nuns resided there more than 20 years earlier. The walls were plain white, and a large wooden Crucifix hung above the dresser. One single red rose stood in a small vase on the desk with a folded handmade sign which read, Welcome Shawn & Laura with two red hearts. Though the room itself didn't rise to the romantic notion I had envisioned with a fireplace, wine, and loveseat, the flower and note were a nice touch.

At six o'clock sharp, we arrived at the meeting room which hosted at least 20 other married couples. I felt relieved to see no familiar faces, as I didn't want people we knew to find out our marriage was in trouble. I was too private and image conscious for such a level of exposure. We quietly took a seat near the back as I anxiously awaited to receive the *how-to* to fix my marriage.

After introductions, we tiptoed into the program. The speakers said the crux of what they would cover was slotted for the next day. In the meantime, we learned what would become a valuable tool in our marriage. We learned focused dialogue.

Such discussion meant specific topics and questions we first answered on our own, and then shared with each other. Examples include, "what do I appreciate most about you," "how have you made me sad recently?" and "what is the most difficult situation we are facing as a couple right now?" The list of questions appeared pages long and would give us more than enough ammunition to be united again.

As the first night ended in prayer, the leaders gave us each a notebook with a cover that read, "Love One Another, As I Have Loved You" – John 15:12. It also had a place to write our name and room number. We collected them and went back to our room. As I brushed my teeth, I thought about the wisdom already shared. I wanted what they preached and couldn't wait for the program to begin again in the morning.

The next day started with coffee, pancakes, sausage, and high hopes to turn things around in my marriage. The first session began at 9:00 am, and we dove right into the art of dialogue. We listened to guest speakers share how they overcame failed communication which had almost led them to divorce. Story after story warmed my heart, not because they experienced heartache, but because they found a way to overcome it.

There is no doubt God intervened and led us to that retreat. It turned out the art of dialogue saved our marriage too. It became a habit which lasted for years and opened communication lines we never knew we could have.

At the closing of the retreat, we were encouraged to write each other a short letter, expressing our feelings of our time spent together. Shawn wrote: "*My Sweet Pumpkin Pie, words are not designed to say what my heart and soul feel for you. If I could put our love into perspective, I would use fine crystal. Hard, beautiful, heavy, yet full of light, sparklingly and clear. Forged by fire and crafted by skill. Tough enough to survive a fall, but fragile to the touch. Able to hold what is precious, or common. Our love, forever. I love you and forever I give you my soul, Shawn.*"

Mine, though not as poetic: "*To my love, my life, how wonderful to have such a beautiful man to spend the rest of my life with. I've had such an unforgettable weekend with you and I'll never ever forget it as long as I live. I love you more every day and I am so grateful God brought us together after all the pain we went through in our past. Thank you for supporting this retreat and I thank you for being such a wonderful, loving, heartfelt and awesome husband. Our hearts will be together forever. I love you, Laura."*

And with that, we drove home with our renewed love and a determination to make our marriage work and beat the odds that forever seemed stacked against us.

CHAPTER FOURTEEN

I am Redeemed

By the time Keenan entered first grade, we were burning the candle at both ends. We bought our first (and only) house located in the heart of the city. Built in 1920; some friends and family remarked it was a lovely *starter* home. We fell head over heels before even crossing the threshold.

It sported a picket fence, a flowery trellis entry into a vegetable garden, flower boxes below every window on the first floor and two towering redbud trees that I knew Shawn would decorate with Christmas tree lights. And that was just the outside! Once we passed through the front door, we knew it had to be home.

We made an offer that the seller accepted. Before the ink was even dry on closing day, we sprung from the cushioned office chairs and raced over to our new castle to celebrate with Champagne in hand. Upon entering the back door that leads to the kitchen, we observed a hand towel that the seller placed on the handle of the stove. It had the words, "Welcome Home." What a nice gesture, I thought.

From that time, even to the present day, we've tirelessly worked on renovations. Ugly paint adorned every nook and cranny, including the wood trim and doors throughout the house. Even more hideous was the laminate that covered the kitchen and dining room floors and a shaggy blue carpet elsewhere.

Uncovering the hidden beauty in each room became a favorite hobby for Shawn and myself. It was hard work; heat guns, scrapers, chemicals, and every penny we could spare, and many we could not.

During the week, we were on the lookout for weekend estate sales. The local newspaper sat patiently on the counter with big red circles around the notifications that listed antiques for sale. We became obsessed with old furniture, and like each room in our house, we uncovered the hidden beauty of each gem we found. Menard's (hardware and building supplies) became a home away from home.

As I finished my Associate's Degree, I developed a love for writing. Almost every elective class I registered for related to communication, oral, and written. I enjoyed writing about topics that were close to my heart. It felt freeing to share my thoughts about family, God, and my view of politics. I'd type for hours on our Compaq Presario and saved each masterpiece (or so I thought they were) on a floppy disk so that I could print out the pages in the school computer lab.

In the spring of 1997, I received my first college degree in Supervisory Management with High Honors. As I made my way past the row of temporary metal folding chairs, I adjusted the tassel on my flat square hat so that the Dean could flip it to the side that signified I earned my diploma.

Like salt and pepper, my college graduation was as different from my high school graduation. For starters, the journey to the stage this time around didn't involve unprotected sex that led to abortion, nor did it include hopping from one college to another, and banned from the very man I married. Rather, it was hard earned, and I felt pretty darn accomplished as the cheers from my family sounded like music in my ears.

The next semester, I enrolled at a Catholic University. This time I was going after a Bachelor of Science in Organizational Communication. I didn't know it yet, but this pursuit would yank and tear away all the dark walls guarded by my demons. The next several years would become more than a goal to earn a bigger paycheck. I would be challenged to confront my true feelings about abortion and take a stand on it one way or the other. For it, or against it. Truth be told.

The seeds started in a Philosophy and Values class. No different from the community college, I was the oldest student in class; thus, the other younger students looked at me differently. Was it that obvious that I was 30 years old? I thought I looked young for my age, especially when I split my hair into pigtails and wore the latest jeans from the Gap. Most students looked to me for the wisdom they thought I had in my old age. Questions abound during many a break time.

As expected in a university setting, my assignments became more advanced and involved a lot of research. I was amazed by how many resources were available to validate, enhance or dispute a topic. The internet wasn't as vast at the time as it is today, so I spent many hours either in the public or school libraries. Further research ignited my passion for writing.

For Philosophy and Values, one of the assignments included a research paper that would give me almost half my grade. The professor encouraged us to dig deep and pull out a topic which needed to be value-laden and worthy of our time. How could I not choose abortion? When I shared aloud my choice, the other students looked at me as if to say, "Done and done, many times – what a lame choice!" I ignored them and took abortion as my topic.

As the saying goes, "Knowledge is power," and my research into abortion validated this adage. I'd learn soon enough why ghosts still haunted me about my past. When my discoveries became almost too much to stomach, I wondered if I was going too far with my research. Did I want to know the ins and outs of an abortion clinic? Did I want to know all the gruesome ways used to murder an unborn baby? All the understanding in the world couldn't reverse what I had done at 16 & 17. Why bother?

One study I came across concluded that women who had an abortion had a 50% greater risk of getting breast cancer. Furthermore, if she had one before 18 years of age, the risk was even higher. Shit, I had two before turning 18! Other risk factors were as scary: post-traumatic stress syndrome, alcohol & drug abuse, shame and guilt, suicidal tendencies. At the age of 30, I already could check-off alcohol abuse, shame, and guilt. Over the years, I even considered ending my life. And I am sure I'd been suffering from the stress syndrome for the past 14 years, as one element is depression.

As I thought about my life since that first abortion, I began to understand that perhaps my mood swings and depression, my social anxiety and heavy alcohol use; all was likely related to the trauma of my abortions. Analytically speaking, this made sense to me.

Before this research, my feelings about my abortions were a nuisance; something I had to get over. But you can't do this if you are unaware there are possible long-term effects that don't disappear at the snap of your fingers. I may not have been able to stop the abortions from occurring because of my circumstances at the time; however, my parents and I could have been given the heads-up for mental hang-ups that camped out and invaded my mind for too many years. Maybe such knowledge would have sparked a discussion for the need of counseling?

Instead of feeling release from all that I learned about abortion, I became more frustrated and angry. All at once, I displaced blame directly onto my parents. How could they have let me, even encouraged me, to go through such an ordeal? Did they know what happened to my babies after the procedures? Did they know my risk of suicide?

Certainly not. They knew only of the convenience of the event, not the aftermath, I reasoned. Heads were going to roll now, and since my dad lived in Florida, my vitriol got directed squarely at my mom. Fired up, I got into my car to pay her a visit (Allan and my mom moved back from Indiana by this time). I was hankering for an apology and a detail explanation for why she put me through pure hell.

Mom saw me drive up and came out to the driveway. She looked puzzled by my unannounced visit. Without giving her a chance to say a word, I blurted out, "How could you have let those awful people kill my babies?" I went on and on, playing a victim to a tee. I yelled that I'd been to hell and back and I blamed her, dad, Allan, and Paula.

She just stood there and took it. She didn't stop me. After a while, it didn't feel so good to rant without any rant back. So I stopped shouting. Nothing seemed different. My heart still hurt. My shame and guilt didn't disappear. I drove 50 miles, for what? To toss blame elsewhere, like this could solve my woes?

As we stood in the driveway in a moment of silence, I leaned back against my car, shrugged my shoulders and hung my head. I started to feel sorry for yelling at my mom. She asked, "Where is this coming from? Why are you dredging up the past?" As tears escaped and ran down my cheeks, I knew that no matter how much bellowing I did, neither she, nor my dad or other family members could understand why I couldn't leave well enough alone.

I didn't have the magic words to help her figure out why I felt the need to exhume my buried past. Truth be told, I didn't know why I was compelled to uncover and expose such heartache. Therefore, I said nothing more; I apologized for being so mean, hugged her, and headed back home.

On the drive back, I rolled down the windows on both sides and let the crisscross noise of the wind and the snap of cold on my face take my mind off the last hour of my life. I pushed play on the CD player and added more distraction as I listened to the 90s mix that Shawn recently burned for me. Perfect, Third Eye Blind's Semi-Charmed Life played. "I want something else to get me through this life, baby." This song made me want to drink a bottle or two, of wine.

Next was One Sweet Day by Mariah Carey and Boyz II Men. It's one of those sad songs I could be drawn to in the right mood, even though I cry most times listening to the lyrics. It begins, "Sorry I never told you, all I wanted to say, now it's too late to hold you, 'cause you've flown away." As tears burst from my eyes, I searched for a Kleenex and could not reach one with only one hand on the wheel. So I used my sleeve to wipe away the tears and snot.

It was too late for so many things. Too late to use protection and not get pregnant. Too late to tell the truth and change the outcome and fate of my unborn children. Too late to hold them and love them and care for them. This topic for my school paper was too close to home and now seemed destined for a failing grade. Thus, failing the class altogether.

By the time I got home, I was exhausted emotionally. I wasn't much in the mood to be around Shawn and the kids. Thankfully, they were already involved in activities, and I could sneak away and not be missed. It was late enough in the afternoon to drink, so I opened a bottle of wine.

My mind was on information overload as all of my research, peppered with my actual life experiences and my mom's reaction to my accusations swarmed around in my head. I hated that I could not organize all of it in a neat spiral notebook.

There had to be an easier way to put my past behind me; I thought as I opened bottle #2. As my mind started to blur with each gulp of the intoxicating red beverage I was consuming, my old friends; shame and guilt joined me. I reminded myself that Shawn and I were the ones that lied and hid our sexual relationship all those years. We were the ones that had unprotected sex. It was our fault, no one else.

Like counting sheep to fall asleep, I counted all the ways I screwed up, and as usual, in those days, I fell fast asleep. Not from finding peace in my thoughts, rather from being so drunk; I passed out.

As I finished my research paper, titled, "Abortion is Immoral and should be Illegal," I knew I stood on the right side of the issue. Yet it made me feel so dirty and deceptive. Like a blowhard spouting words that have no exact meaning. My typed sentiments condemned the very thing I had done 14 years ago. Hypocrite, this is what I had become.

I told myself that no one had to know that I had two abortions, ever. Fourteen years was a long time ago, and I was ignorant in those days. Now I was educated and gained a new perspective. This is all that mattered, right? Yes, I reasoned. I felt that the best way to move forward was to keep my secret history hidden. And I was good at keeping secrets, at least for a period. My new mantra became: do as I say, not as I have done.

"Abortion is Immoral and Should be Illegal" earned me an A. One remark from my professor included, "Very insightful." No kidding, the paper is about my personal experience, I silently commented back. The research made it easier to proclaim where I stood in an educated fashion.

Had my teacher known that a majority of my paper included personal experience, I am confident he would have called it biased. However, he didn't need to know about my past, no one did. As long as he and everyone else never found out about my past sins, I would not be a hypocrite, at least on the outside where I thought it mattered.

Based on my addictive nature, I couldn't stop reinventing myself to be a real pro-life woman, which is what I was slowing becoming. I became a member of a right to life group and learned even more about abortion through anecdotal stories told by other members at meetings and conventions.

Sitting in the audience, I became riveted by the stories of how abortion all but killed the brave women that stood tall behind the podium. It was hard not to cry because I could relate each story to my story. The main difference was that the speakers gave their pain over to Jesus and learned to heal through God's grace and forgiveness. I had not done this, at least not yet. I wanted to reach redemption, as proclaimed is the ultimate prize.

Meanwhile, my marriage, family, and school life forged ahead full speed. Shawn and the kids were none the wiser to the angst I was knee deep and drowning in. I didn't want to burden them and put a kink in the façade of our perfect family life. I began to drink more, and I spent most of my downtime alone. I figured that if I kept to myself, I was less likely to reveal that I felt broken and did not know how to fix myself.

Thankfully, Shawn is a hands-on dad. He picked up the slack that I left behind daily. I was minimally engaged in our family activities and performed only the must-mom duties like laundry and shopping. After that, I checked out and became desolate. Typically, I'd make an excuse that I had homework to get done, and I would drink until I couldn't remember my pain any longer.

On one of those nights, I attempted to make it up the stairs to go to bed. As I tried to keep the focus on each baby step ahead, I didn't notice my family watching television in the living room. Unsteady on my feet, I tripped on the first set of stairs, and the kids rushed over to see if I was okay.

As they stood over me, they both peppered me with comments as I awkwardly sat on a stair, unable to move with any composure. Among other things, they said that I drank too much and that they didn't want to see me get hurt. I laughed off their concerns, turned myself around and crawled up each step till I reached the top; all the while my kids following behind to make sure I got in bed safely.

Like a nightmare, I woke the next morning trying to remember the details of what unfolded. I could recall tidbits, like my kids were crying about my behavior. But everything else was a blur. It seemed like I merely existed to play the shell of wife and mother, and to an extent, student. And it was all shadowed by a hanging fog that would not lift and bring forth sunshine.

Thankfully, it was the weekend. As I watched the ceiling fan go round and around, I tried to figure out if I should gloss over last night and pretend it didn't happen. Or, if I should finally tell my family that I needed help. The choice was made for me when we congregated at the kitchen table for breakfast.

In a cute and concerned fashion, my family staged a mini-intervention. Shawn started it out by saying he was worried I was drinking a lot and that I wasn't smiling much anymore. The kids echoed his thoughts and added that they didn't want me to die from alcohol poisoning. There was nothing cute about what they were telling me, and I became embarrassed and ashamed. I also had a raging headache from the two bottles of wine I drank the night before.

I had a hard time getting any words out; what kind of mother had I become? I was spending so much time grieving the loss of my two aborted babies; all the while taking for granted that God gave me two more that were alive and standing right in front of me. If ever there was a come to Jesus moment, it was at that low point, standing in the kitchen while my pancakes were getting cold.

Somehow I had to pull myself together. I could not allow my past to define and destroy me and ultimately my family. Shawn knew I was struggling with my abortions because we had been talking on and off about my research for several weeks. But our children knew nothing about my past sins and the thought of them finding out was almost too much to bear.

The mini-intervention got my attention though, and I promised to try to stop drinking so much and spend more time with my family. I wanted to reach the same peace that those women had at the conferences. I was at a crossroads, and I needed to find a path that could lead me to redemption.

In a roundabout way, one of our parish priests had learned about my pro-life passion. After Mass one Sunday, I shared with him the story of Kayla and how a close friend wanted me to abort her. I told him how much joy she had brought me and that I never regretted my decision. Keeping in touch with the hypocrisy of my pro-life stance, I didn't share the *other* pregnancy stories with him.

Father asked if I would be willing to share my story with the congregation in an upcoming Mass. He said he was looking for parishioners to give an account of a genuine experience; something that is uplifting and inspiring. He told me that my story fits the bill. I said I would be happy to share my story and raced to catch up with Shawn and the kids as they had begun walking home.

On the rest of the walk home, I didn't mention to Shawn what Father had asked. Instead, I batted around the hypocrisy notion and wondered if it was even ethical to leave out the abortion stories. When we got home, the kids scattered to their bedrooms and I told Shawn about Father's request. As usual, he was encouraging and said that God put such an idea in Father's head for a reason. The request ultimately came from God.

He helped me sketch an outline of the speech, and I began to see how my story could be worthy of sharing. At age eighteen, I didn't take the easy way out, again. When the choice was mine to make, I chose to give life to my baby. If I had to do it all over again, I would do exactly what I did when I sat in my friend's car on the side of the road. I would tell her, as I did, that I was keeping my baby.

A few weeks later, I stood in front of the congregation and shared my story. I kept my abortions out. They didn't belong in that speech. Instead, I explained how turning to God, and the Catholic Church gave me the courage and hope to bring a baby into the world alone. This is the storyline that mattered. This is the one that changed my life for the better and plopped me on the road that led me to redemption. Though the journey took a long time to travel with many bumps and roadblocks along the way; ultimately I reached the peace those other women had attained.

As I finished my speech, I looked at my family sitting in the front pew. They are all that matter in my story, and I knew from that day on that I could be okay about my past. That morning, as I accepted a standing ovation and thundercloud applause from my fellow parishioners, I vowed I would try not to let my past mistakes define me anymore. I received God's forgiveness, which allowed me to forgive myself and finally feel I could move on. It was time, and it was long overdue.

A few weeks later in the Deep South, I received what I had been after for years. Redemption was mine for the taking, and I accepted it whole-heartedly on that mission trip while attending that old sweltering Baptist Church service with the boisterous Pastor that spoke to me on behalf of my Lord and Savior.

Epilogue by Shawn Eckert

Hello. My name is Shawn Eckert. By this time you have learned a bit about me, and about whom I was once upon a time. Definitely not always a "great" guy. You also know that I am Laura's husband and long-time lover. You also may have gathered how I felt about the subject of abortion once upon a time based on my lackluster involvement when Laura got pregnant during our teenage years together.

What you do not know about is my transformation into a proponent of the pro-life movement, and how that evolution transpired. You also do not know how Laura's journey aided in my motivation to look at abortion differently. When Laura and I moved north to raise our children, we were fortunate to become part of an active Pro-Life community within our Catholic Church. This was just one element of Laura's transformation.

When Laura decided to go to college in the late 1990s, she did so with the goal of earning more money and establishing a new career. She had no idea when she enrolled in college that this endeavor would kick-start her journey to redemption. Laura seemed to devour every bit of knowledge she could acquire. She especially loved her writing classes and the ideas she was exposed to in her theology classes.

Especially interesting to her were the pro-life ideas woven throughout her theology classes, and our Catholic faith. She began to delve deeper into the subject; deeper into the movement. She wrote one of her first and finest papers on the subject of abortion. It was in reviewing and editing one of these papers for her, that I first became exposed to her knowledge and passion for the subject matter. I began to feel the rumblings from my own past start to surface on the matter, and began to realize how much it had affected us individually and as a couple over the years.

During these years, we talked, cried, and even argued about abortion. As Laura learned more about the after-effects of abortion, she began to drink a lot and displayed other uncharacteristic behaviors such as isolation and short-temperateness.

I too began to write on the subject of abortion when I returned to school. However, I had an entirely different angle and scope on the subject.

I got to thinking about the father's side of abortion. Men have never had much of any voice or impact on the outcome of their partner's decision to abort their pregnancy.

I've come to understand that men have no power when it comes to the "choice" of abortion or life. We are legally impotent when it comes to defending the life of an unborn child. The more stories I read of men being shut-out of this life-altering decision, the more I began to take this injustice personally.

I wondered why men have no voice when it comes to their unborn children. Is an unborn baby not just as much a part of their father as their mother? Why is it only the body of the woman that is considered in this "choice" and not the emotional well-being of the father as well? Throughout the years I've spoken to many men who have echoed these questions and shared a reminiscence of powerlessness to defend their unborn child.

I have listened to the frustration they express as they recollect a complete denial of any voice, and the falseness of claims that a majority of the time, abortion is a convenience for men.

Nonsense. Abortion is not looked at in this society through the lens of a significant, life-altering, sometimes dangerous medical procedure. It is in fact, considered as a final convenience for a woman, regardless of the expressed wishes of the man involved.

This is not to say that some women don't have to face this arduous decision alone. Far too many women do. It is simply to say that men have always been and remain completely voiceless as court rulings have upheld and perpetuated this understanding.

It's been a very long and difficult road to watch Laura reach a point where she doesn't cry when our unborn babies come to mind. For every time she has cried, I remember them too and cry as well.

When Laura started writing about her journey years ago, I hoped and prayed it would culminate in this very publication. Just like years before, with her college papers, I reviewed and helped edit this book. As I read each chapter, I experienced a dark and painful recollection of not only Laura's journey, but mine too.

I hope her story helps other women who are or have experienced similar circumstances as a result of abortion. I also hope that the men who read this story can appreciate the fragility that cannot be understated and understand that they too may need to find healing and redemption. Much of my healing journey involves a very caring therapist that I've seen for years. However, there are many other resources available for men that are seeking help for abortion healing.

As the father of remarkable human beings, I mourn that I never had the chance to hear two of those children's beautiful voices. I mourn that I had a hand in them never getting the chance to hear mine, to hold my finger, to hug me, to smile, to play under the sun.

I mourn that at one time in my life I was far too immature and selfish to care about their voices.

I know one day when I see them in heaven that I will be able to hold them as if I was never apart from them. And a glorious day it will be!

Letter to my Unborn Babies

To my never forgotten unborn children,

I am so very sorry for not bringing you into this world. I was young and reckless and never considered the consequences that led me to Planned Parenthood to end your lives.

I have so much regret from my younger years, I've faltered in ways that are so shameful. I dream of you often and honestly believe that I will see you someday in Heaven. I know that God has been watching over you and taking the very best care of you. I cannot change the past, but if I could, you would have been held in my arms and showered with kisses and deep love and affection.

I believe that you have forgiven me and that you love me. And I want you to know that I kept asking God to forgive me over and over again. I did it because while I wanted it, I never actually felt worthy of his forgiveness or love because of what I had done to you. Years later, I finally accepted that He had forgiven me when I asked the first time. He is a loving and forgiving God and Father, and I needed to seek forgiveness only once. It took me years to understand this.

But I had a lot of emotions and heartache to deal with, and it took me a long time to reach a point in my healing process where I could accept what I did and try to live a life that was more pleasing to God. It has been a long, difficult and at times very painful journey to getting these words typed to you. I believe that you know this to be true as I feel you are with me in spirit every second of every day. I also believe that you are aware that I am a changed person from the reckless and tragic days of my youth.

I used to fear meeting you because I could only imagine seeing the pain and sorrow in your eyes. But now I am looking forward to being reunited with you forevermore because I know that beyond a shadow of a doubt that you are as healed and whole as I am now.

I love you so very much.

All my love, Mom

Special Acknowledgement

A BIG shout-out to my very dear friend and cherished confidant, Kim Carr!

Kim has been instrumental in helping me reach publication and has dug into every sentence of my book and provided valuable content editing and advice. When I experienced apprehension about sharing particular content, she always had the right wisdom for me. I will forever be grateful for the endless hours she spent pouring over the pages and the constructive feedback that followed. I treasure our friendship and her love and support immensely.

Notes

Whether you find yourself in a pregnancy crisis or if you have experienced an abortion and you seek healing; many helpful resources and organizations exist today. Regardless of the city size you live in, you will likely find help right in your own community. If you cannot locate any, the internet has an incredible amount of information that may be useful and helpful to you. I have had personal experience with the resources below.

Crisis Pregnancy Homes

When I was in graduate school, I was part of a team that was assigned an "Organizational Analysis Project" in the context of a final assessment for graduation. Our goal was to utilize strategic planning methods gleaned from various resources that could provide actual steps for improving the overall health of an organization.

We chose a non-profit pregnancy home in Fond du Lac, WI because of various shortcomings it was experiencing. It was during this time that I learned how impactful these types of homes are for women in a crisis pregnancy. Most importantly, I learned that women seeking shelter are not judged because of their circumstance. Rather, they are welcomed and treated with respect and dignity.

Crisis pregnancy homes are typically operated by an Executive Director and a host of volunteers. Women that become residents of the home are taught healthy parenting and essential life skills. These homes utilize a network of professional and community resources to aid in providing counseling, health and nutrition education, adoption information (if so desired), and preparation for independent living.

Assistance from pregnancy homes does not end when a baby is born. Rather, post-residents can continue to utilize the professional and community resources that were available when they were a resident of the home. There is an on-going commitment to foster successful independent living and parenting skills.

To locate a nearby home, type: Crisis Pregnancy Home or Center in a web search and you will likely find a few web links to begin your search.

Abortion Healing

There are so many excellent resources available for women seeking to heal from an abortion. When I first realized that I was suffering from my abortion experiences and needed help, I searched for books that offered a roadmap to recovery. Two books that helped me the most:

- Beyond the Hidden Pain of Abortion by Patricia A. Bigliardi (1994).
- Changed, Making Sense of Your Own or Loved One's Abortion Experience by Michaelense Fredenburg (2008).

Many Churches have ministries that offer judgement-free meetings, support groups, and one-on-one counseling when seeking healing and forgiveness. As a Catholic, I am aware of and have utilized "**Project Rachel**" over the years.

This is an online resource: http://hopeafterabortion.com.

The **National Right to Life** is an incredible resource. Under the "Pregnant?" tab, you will find information to help you locate a Pregnancy Resource Center nearby and other links that can assist you as you begin your healing journey. This also is an online resource: http://www.nrlc.org.

Focus on the Family is another resource that I used extensively when I was in the throes of searching for redemption. Please visit www.focusonthefamily.com for more information.

In recent years, I mostly listen to Christian music and glean a plethora of inspiring messages from many songs. In the past year, I have found three songs that have become my favorites because they relate to my story on a very personal level:

- Family Tree by Matthew West
- Prodigal by the Sidewalk Prophets
- Redeemed by Big Daddy Weave

Lastly, I highly recommend Joyce Meyer's book, "Do Yourself a Favor...Forgive, Learn How to Take Control of Your Life Through Forgiveness." (2012)

Laura Eckert

Laura was born and raised in Wisconsin. She has been married to Shawn since 1989 and has two adult children. She is a first-time author and hopes to partner with Shawn shortly to write a Memoir about their youth mission trip experiences. Laura's greatest love is God and family. Her hobbies include writing, genealogy and trying to emulate crafty projects found on Pinterest.

Please visit Lauraeckertbooks.com to learn more about Laura and her family.

Made in the USA
Lexington, KY
24 June 2017